HOW TO
BUILD YOUR ART
BUSINESS
WITH LIMITED TIME OR ENERGY

By Corrina Thurston

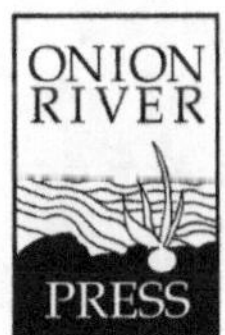

Onion River Press
191 Bank Street
Burlington, Vermont 05401

Onion River Press
191 Bank Street
Burlington, VT 05401

Printed in the United States of America

ISBN: 978-1-949066-10-4

Library of Congress Control Number: 2018957595

To my family and loved ones for your constant support.

I couldn't do any of this without you.

What Others Are Saying About HOW TO BUILD YOUR ART BUSINESS WITH LIMITED TIME OR ENERGY....

"I just finished reading Corrina Thurston's book HOW TO BUILD YOUR ART BUSINESS WITH LIMITED TIME OR ENERGY for the second time and I can honestly say that my life would be very different now if I'd had this manual to build an art career in my 20's! That being said, in the spirit of "never too late," I will be implementing the many guidelines and pointers she has laid out so plainly in this very smart guide.

That Corrina was able to build a successful art career, essentially from zero (starting to draw from her sickbed to keep busy) to creating quality art, exhibitions, writing and getting grants, collaborations and more is inspirational.

Need a boost for your career? You will likely find the roadmap here, and enjoy the journey!"

– Susan Donze

"Corrina Thurston shares her hard won knowledge and guidance in a friendly, conversational style. She doesn't hold anything back, and every page contains useful information and ideas."

– Kelly Paquet

"Corrina Thurston's ebook entitled, How to Build Your Art Business with Limited Time or Energy, is a must read! Miss Thurston discusses many topics of interest including: Having the Right Goals, Creating a Business Plan, Multiple Streams of Income, Email Marketing, and Branding. She also wrote a bonus section which includes, 12 Questions to ask before creating a Partnership. I found her book extremely informative."

– Lisa Perfetti

Table Of Contents:

BONUS MATERIALS:

1
Dear Reader

Dear Reader,

The main goal of this book is to help you be more productive and prioritize the activities that will move your business forward, create a bigger audience for your work, and get you more sales/income from your artwork and art-related products and services, despite what time or energy limitations you may have.

This book will help anyone starting or struggling with their art business, but it is especially helpful for those with limited time or energy to spare.

To give you a little background about me, I'm a professional artist working out of Vermont, USA, and I have a chronic illness. Actually, I have multiple chronic health problems and they limit what I can do and when I can do it. This is especially problematic in trying to run and grow a business, so I've learned techniques to maximize my productivity when I'm feeling well enough, and make my business work for me by prioritizing things that will grow my business without getting overwhelmed.

I know there are things I can't do because of my health limitations, so I avoid them and focus my energy and time on the things I *can* do.

This book can help you focus your energy on what works for your business, grow your audience, gain more customers, create more income (including passive income), and optimize your efforts.

If I can do it, I believe you can too.

2
Ask Yourself These Questions

No business can succeed unless you have a focus. Therefore, one of the first things you need to do is to ask yourself these 8 questions below. I'll go into more detail about some of them further down, and the rest in upcoming chapters.

1.) What is the number one priority for your business? (To make art? To be represented by galleries? To make an income/provide a living? To teach people your skills? To spread a message? Etc.)

2.) Who is your ideal audience/customer? (Harder to answer than it seems sometimes!)

3.) What's your focus/niche?

4.) Are you mission-oriented and working towards a specific cause?

5.) Who are the influential companies/people in your field?

6.) What are your limitations? (Are you chronically ill, in chronic pain, have a full-time day job, have kids you take care of, etc.)

7.) Where do you want your business to go? (Financially, within your field, expansion, will you have a team of employees? etc.)

8.) And what do you need to do to get there?

Some of these questions will be easier to answer than others, and some will require research. Your ideal audience can be especially tricky for artists. If you make baby clothing, then your ideal audience is an easier question to answer: parents of babies! But maybe you can go even further than that. Is your baby clothing mostly sports-oriented? Then your ideal audience is parents of babies who also love sports.

But what about when you make abstract paintings? Or ceramics? Or sculpture, or drawings? Who's your ideal customer then?

Our knee-jerk reaction is to say that our artwork appeals to everyone! That's part of why it's so great! But that answer is going to work against your business as you try to build. The more focused you can be on your answer to this, the better off you are when it comes to marketing and attracting new customers.

I have particular difficulty with this question. I'm a wildlife artist and I specialize in detailed, vibrant portraits of animals. So when it comes to figuring out my audience, in the beginning I was keeping track of who was commenting and liking my artwork on social media and in person. The age range was everyone. It appealed to both genders. It was across the spectrum for people's age, race, class, etc. It was literally *everyone*.

What I realized, however, is that even though it appealed to what seemed like everyone, not everyone was buying it.

So I changed my thinking. My artwork appeals to "everyone," but my ideal customer happens to be a woman age 30-60, who is an animal lover, realism art lover, and likely to support wildlife conservation or at least have an interest in wildlife more than the average person. This is based on closely watching who was actually buying my artwork, and making a conscious effort to bring wildlife conservation into my business because it's something I'm passionate about.

That also goes into the question of whether or not your business is going to be connected to a cause and be mission-based.

I decided it would be easier and better to brand my company as one that works towards a cause I care about: wildlife conservation. This gives me the opportunity to not only support a worthy cause, but also show customers that I'm working toward something bigger than myself, and it gives me the opportunity to work with other people and companies with a similar mission.

As you think about some of the questions above, you're already on your way to building your business. To do so successfully, you're going to want to think about where you want your business to go. This connects to what type of business you want to be, as in: Is making money your number one priority? Is spreading knowledge your priority? Is helping a cause your priority? Is getting your artwork in prestigious galleries your priority?

Any of the above make perfectly fine priorities for your business. One is not any better or worse than the other. There's nothing wrong with wanting to make money from what you do, despite the stigma that sometimes comes with that confession. Nor is there anything wrong with wanting to focus on teaching or becoming an expert in your field, or being in prestigious galleries. Every person is going to have their own motivation that drives them to do this business.

The question then is: How do I get there? How do I start a business and build it up to be successful, especially if I only have a limited amount of time or energy to devote to it? That's what this book is about, and it all starts with your goals.

3
Having The Right Goals

Goals are an important part of a successful business, especially if you have limited time or energy to focus on building it up. You want to know exactly where you're going with your business and how to get there.

The problem is when people don't make the right goals and it stunts their business and especially their productivity.

The biggest problems with most goals are:
- People make them too lofty
- They're not measurable
- People don't follow through with them
- They're overwhelming
- They're the wrong goals

Making Your Goals Too Lofty:

Many times when you ask someone what their business goals are, they respond with something about getting into a prestigious gallery, becoming well-known, making lots of money, etc. The problem with these goals is that they're not very specific and they're too lofty, especially if you're just starting out or if you have limited time.

It's a good thing to have ideas like this in the back of your mind as something to drive you in your business, but these are not your goals. These are things you might aspire to, but they're not going to help you grow your business and there's no clear path on how to get there.

Goals That Aren't Measurable:

If you want to have success in reaching your goals, they have to be measurable. What does that mean? It means you need to be able to tell if you're getting close to reaching your goal and know when you have. Saying your goal is to become well-known doesn't work. What does well-known mean? How would you know if you achieved it?

Instead, make your goal more specific, like I want to have 10,000 followers on social media, or I want to have 1,000 people on my email list. This way you can measure exactly how close you are to your goal and you can keep track of which efforts are helping you achieve it and which aren't.

Not Following Through With Your Goals:

Sometimes you have a goal in mind and you just don't follow through. I'm guilty of this at times and I think everyone is at one point or another. Especially if your goals are too overwhelming (see below). This can either be because you don't have the right goals, they're too overwhelming, you're procrastinating, or other things keep getting in the way.

If you have a goal that you've written down but you don't seem to be doing anything about it for one reason or another, maybe it's not as important as you think. What would happen if you erased that goal and replaced it with another one? Or, if you know that goal is important, but it's just something you're dreading, like bookwork, try to figure out what you can do to motivate yourself. Should you give yourself a reward afterward for completing it? Should you work on it in smaller chunks? Can you get help with it?

Goals That Are Overwhelming:

This is one of the most common problems with goals! If I were to ask a room of people starting their art business to write down their immediate goals, most of them would say things like: getting artwork in galleries or retailers, a solo exhibit, getting their work published, teaching a workshop, etc.

These are all great things to work for, but if you write down on your whiteboard under goals, *a solo exhibit*, when you look at it each day what do you do? Do you get overwhelmed? How do you know how to proceed or what should be done to get there?

The problem isn't that you have a bad goal. It's a great goal! The problem is that this is a Summit Goal and you need Step Goals in order to climb to reach it.

A Summit Goal is an overarching goal. It's still measurable and reachable, but it involves a lot of smaller steps in order to achieve it. Therefore, you need Step Goals. Step Goals are all those smaller steps you need to take in order to get there.

For example, if your Summit Goal is to have a solo exhibit, some of your Step Goals might be:

- Research local galleries to decide which 5 typically display artwork similar to my own (don't waste time applying to galleries that specialize in abstract artwork if you're a portrait artist!)
- Research who curates those qualifying galleries
- Create a proposal for each gallery
- Choose a title and theme for my exhibit
- Choose and format images of artwork
- Create a disc or flash drive of properly formatted images
- Write a cover letter specific to each gallery
- Revise and print my resume/CV
- Create a clean, professional presentation (things are printed, not handwritten, a nice folder possibly with your branding on it, artwork covering the disc or a flash drive, quality paper and printing, include a business card, etc.)
- Make an appointment to drop off proposal

- Go drop off proposal
- Follow up with curators 5 days after dropping off the proposal to make sure they got it if you didn't hand it to them directly, or wait 2-3 weeks to check in with them if you did see them directly
- Keep researching other galleries to potentially send proposals

You can see how that one goal turned into a number of Step Goals as we broke it down.

The smaller your goals, the easier they are to meet.

This is important for productivity. Some of you won't need to break your goals down as much as I did above, but some of you will. I like to break everything down so I can continue to cross them off and move on to the next one. What you're doing here is outlining your process.

For anyone who's a writer, you may know from experience how useful an outline can be for organizing your thoughts and streamlining a process. The more organized your thoughts are going into a project and the more you have it planned out, the easier and quicker it'll be to complete it.

Some people, like me, also like the feeling of crossing items off our list and feeling productive in smaller chunks. If your goal is too big and it's taking you days or weeks to complete it, that can be draining. You feel like you're not getting anywhere, even though you are. With the list of Step Goals, you have specific things you know you've accomplished, and you can see just how many more things you'll need to do to reach your Summit Goal.

The more you break a goal down, the less daunting it will seem. Saying you want to get your work into 10 regional retailers is a great Summit Goal, but it's a daunting task. Thinking about it as a single goal may make you anxious and feel overwhelmed, like it's too big to tackle. But if you break it down into Step Goals, it won't seem as daunting.

Every once in a while you'll have a goal that you think is a Step Goal, but for some reason you're still finding it overwhelming. For instance, in the above example of Step Goals for the solo exhibit, you might write down 'make proposals' as one of your step goals. Then as you get to that goal, you start finding yourself getting anxious and like it's too big a goal for you to tackle in one step, so you break it down into smaller steps, like I did above.

The Wrong Goals:

Unfortunately, sometimes you just have the wrong goals. If you want to gain a Facebook following of 10,000 people, then your goals need to be relevant to that idea. You can't expect followers to pop out of the air just because you donated a piece of artwork to a cause. HOWEVER, if you donate to a cause and then have them promote your donation on their Facebook page, with a link to yours, and you post on their page in a complimentary way, that could bring you some followers, especially if you've chosen an organization that has a lot of *active* followers themselves.

If your goal is to be published and to do that you're trying to get lots of gallery attention, your goals may be wrong. What you may need to do, depending on the publication, is send proposals to them directly, or enter a contest, or reach out to one of their editors.

Every goal should have a direct purpose that leads you closer to a Summit Goal. And your Summit Goals should each lead you closer to your number 1 priority for your business.

If it's not taking your business forward, it shouldn't be one of your goals.

4
Learning To Prioritize

Especially if you have limited time or energy, prioritizing is going to be extremely important. You have limited time, so you need to focus on the most important parts of your business. But how do you decide what's most important?

The first and easiest way to prioritize what you have to do is by deadline. Whatever deadline is closest means that should be a priority. That's just common sense, but a lot of people don't follow it and then they're scrambling to get something done.

The other way to figure out your priorities is to think back about what your number one priority is for your business. If your number one priority is to make a living from your artwork or craft, then the best thing you can do is prioritize activities that will make you money, especially passive income. Income is great, but passive income is even better (see later chapter on multiple streams of income).

If your goal is to make art every day, then you should prioritize your creation of artwork. Just keep in mind that if you don't spend time marketing your artwork, the business won't grow.

Just having beautiful artwork unfortunately won't make a successful business.

The point is, if you only have a certain amount of time,

prioritize things that will truly enhance your business and move you forward and stop spending time on things that don't.

Some ways you can prioritize and help remind yourself which things need to be done are:

- Set reminders on your phone
- Make a chart of tasks
- Use a whiteboard

Set Reminders On Your Phone Or Device:

Phones, tablets, and computers now have the ability to set reminders, calendar dates, or time yourself with a simple app. This means if you need to do these things to help you prioritize, you have help! If you want to make sure you only spend an hour on research, or 3 hours drawing, you can set an alarm for yourself to make sure you stick to that schedule. If you want to remind yourself that there's a deadline for a competition or an event happening, you can put it on your phone when you think of it and have it remind you when you need it.

Make A Chart For Tasks:

Sometimes you need to figure out exactly what's most important for you to accomplish first, second, and third. A good way to do that is to make a chart.

NEED: **SHOULD:**   **WANT:**

One of my favorite charts to help myself figure out what is most important is the **Need**, **Should**, **Want** chart. Under the **Need** category I write in the things that absolutely need to be done, especially things that have an upcoming deadline.

In the **Should** category goes everything I know would be good for me to do and good for my business, but aren't as necessary or as deadline-specific as the **Need** category.

In the **Want** category goes everything else I want to do for my business, but isn't a priority right now.

Here's an example of some things I have in my chart for this week:

NEED:	SHOULD:	WANT:
Art Hop (deadline)	Write In Book	Clean Studio
Ale Contest(deadline)	Plan Series	Rhino Drawing
Commission	Ask Bloggers	Wire Sculpture
Ship Last Comm.	Proposal To Gallery	Brochures
File S.Tax(deadline)	Buy Prints For Exhibit	
Pack/Ship Orders	Send Thank You Notes	

Use A Whiteboard:

If you're like me, sometimes you need to have your goals in front of your face in order to focus on them and get them done. That's why you hear some successful entrepreneurs write important notes directly on their bathroom mirror, so they're sure to look at them every day, first thing in the morning.

What I do is use a large whiteboard.

Each day I walk into my studio, my whiteboard is hanging on the wall I'm walking toward. On it are my Summit Goals on the left, and my Step goals for that day or week on the right. As I finish the goals, I get rid of them from the board and move on.

You may not need a whiteboard, but I find it to be a great way to organize my thoughts and goals, and have them staring at me in my studio, judging me if I'm not actively working on them.

The most important piece of advice to take away from the above is:

You need to prioritize the activities that will actually build your business and move you forward.

There's no doubt that sometimes there are tasks that aren't as important that you can and should make time to do. Absolutely. The point is, don't get distracted by those so much that you're not actively moving your business forward and seeing results. If you find that Twitter isn't doing much for you, and yet you spend a half hour a day on Twitter, then you should cut down that time and use it for a bigger priority. If you find you have to respond to a lot of emails and it's taking a lot of your time, but not getting you many sales, maybe you should figure out a way to simplify the process or hire someone to help you.

If you're answering the same questions over and over again in emails, you should have the answers written out somewhere that you can just copy and paste into the emails to respond to people instead of writing it out over and over and over again.

For example, people ask me about commissions all the time, and the answer is pretty complex. So I have it written down in a Word document and every time someone asks me about the process and pricing for a commissioned drawing, I copy and paste it into the email, saving myself a ton of time. Then I simply tweak the response so that it fits exactly what the person is asking about.

I do this for a number of questions that I get over and over again, like what pencils/paper/framing/varnish do I use? Or how long does it take me to complete a drawing?

The other thing you should do is to make sure that you have a page on your website that has FAQs (frequently asked questions). This way, hopefully people see that page before directly asking you the same questions, or if they didn't see it, you can politely direct them to that page instead of having to answer them each and every time.

5

$\mathcal{D}$iscover Your Working Style

Everyone has a different working style. What you need to do is figure out yours so you can optimize your work routine and be as productive as possible.

Do you work better with music playing? In silence? With the TV running? Do you need multiple things going on and prefer working in a bit of chaos? Are you better off being messy and having everything out in front of you, or are you more productive if things are neat and organized?

There's no right way to be productive. Everyone has their own working style, but sometimes we don't realize what that style is. Sometimes you may naturally think that working in silence will help you be more productive and focus, but in reality, you just haven't tried working to music, which can get you pumped and help stave off boredom. Or, the opposite. Some people have something running in the background, thinking they easily get bored if they don't have it, but they haven't tried working in silence, which may be better for them.

Unless you're sure of your own working style, mix it up to see how productive you are in multiple settings, to make sure.

Some people need to have their time scheduled out and others work more from the seat of their pants. Stephen King, for example, sets aside 8am to 12pm every day to write. He doesn't wait to be inspired or find his muse, he just sits down to write every single morning. Sometimes what comes out is great. Other times, it's not. But for his working style, he has a schedule from which he doesn't waver. He learned a long time ago that this was how his brain worked and that he needed to be in the same place each day to be productive, and it shows! He's one of the most productive writers in history.

I would love to be able to work like that, but I learned the hard way that it doesn't work for me. I tried. I desperately wanted to have a schedule that was organized so I knew exactly what I'd be doing each morning, but it made me miserable and my productivity slowed drastically. I felt like if I didn't have a schedule, how could I succeed? What was wrong with me? It made perfect sense that scheduling my time would help me be more productive, but I didn't account for my mind refusing to work that way.

For some people, not scheduling your time is actually better for your productivity.

Some people also work best in chunks. Maybe you work best from 9-5 or working straight through whatever amount of time you have available. Or, maybe you're like me and you're more productive if you get up every half hour or hour to get yourself a drink of water and move around.

Typically after a few hours I start to get drained. This means in the middle of the day it's perfect timing for me to take a break and go outside for a walk. The mixture of being outdoors and the exercise of walking helps lift my spirit, get the blood flowing, and reengage my brain. Once I'm done my half-hour walk I'm back in the studio and ready to get back to work on whatever I was doing (on the days where I have this kind of energy).

As a writer I'm always amazed when I come back to a piece of writing-in-progress and realize I ended in the middle of a sentence. It makes no sense to me and I never do it on purpose. And yet it happens over and over again. Somehow, as I'm writing along I seem to hit a brick wall that stops me no matter what I'm writing and

I stop where I am, with no rhyme or reason. I don't even notice it, I just suddenly realize I need to stop and get up and do something else for a while.

This is how my brain works and I've stopped trying to force it to work in other, more sensible ways. And in doing so, I'm more productive than ever.

What you need to do is learn how your brain works and then manipulate your work schedule around that.

If you're easily distracted from your work and it's digging in to your productivity and efficiency because you're checking your phone (I'm guilty!) or looking at Facebook, then you need to recognize that and make sure you can't get distracted when you're working.

I know some writers who have a sign on their studio door when they're concentrating on their writing and when it's up, no one is allowed to bother them. Their family knows the sign and stays away while they're trying to concentrate and be productive.

There are also programs on your computer or devices where you can block social media from giving you any notifications for whatever time period you want. Or just turn off your Internet completely. I used to have to do this when I was writing or creating advertising/graphic design materials for my business and kept getting distracted. "Ooh, there's a new email that just popped up, maybe it's an acceptance!" Or, "Oh man, I just got 4 notifications on Facebook within a minute, I need to see what's going on!"

No you don't.

At least not during the time period you've set aside to work productively on whatever project you're working on.

Emails and notifications will still be there when you're done, you don't have to view them all immediately.

It may even be beneficial for you to have times of the day when you check your email and social media. Let's say, you check them in the morning to see if there's anything urgent you need to schedule or do for that day, you check them in the middle of the day, and then again late in the afternoon. Maybe you also check them in the evening, but it's up to you how much of your day you want to work and be checking emails. No one expects you to answer an email at 10pm on a Wednesday, so perhaps it can wait until your morning check?

Prioritizing your time like this will help you be way more productive and less distracted. If you have dedicated times to check your email and notifications, you don't need them buzzing your phone and you can focus on the task at hand instead of stopping to check every time an email comes in.

The more you lose focus on a task by checking other things and being distracted, the less efficient and productive you'll be. Checking your email three times a day means you won't miss anything important and nothing urgent will be overlooked.

Checking your emails during those times also helps you break up your day. I know that my brain works best in chunks, meaning I work best in 1-3 hour stints, depending on the project. Sometimes it's best for me to get up every hour to walk and get a drink, get my blood flowing, especially if it's a project that I've been dreading.

I work best when I take breaks, move around, and get fresh air.

Studies have shown that shorter workdays can lead to higher productivity levels, which is the norm in some other countries. The same thing goes for smaller chunks of time.

I'm not saying if you're in the groove and working away on a project that you should necessarily get up and move around, because if you're already being productive you may not need to do that. What I'm saying is if you're starting to lose focus, or you need to reevaluate what you're doing and come at it with fresher eyes, get up and get yourself some tea or water, play with your cat for a few minutes or go for a short walk. Then come back to it. Sometimes it only takes a few minutes.

I find I'm most productive on days when I take a break in the middle of the day to go for a walk. On a good day I tend to drink tea and focus on emails and correspondence in the morning, then move on to a project until I start getting cross-eyed in the mid-day, then go for a brisk walk, maybe a mile or two, then come back and settle in to work on another project or go back to the one I was doing. (Again, this is on days when I have this amount of energy, which is certainly not always with my chronic illnesses. Some days I'm in bed.)

You may not be working a full day and have stricter time restraints. That's okay. Manipulate this trick into smaller chunks for yourself. Instead, maybe you work on a project for an hour or two and then take a break for food or a half-mile walk, and then you get back to it for another hour or two. Just remember if your brain isn't focusing or you're struggling to get something done, you may need to move around some or work on a different project altogether.

There are times you should force yourself to work on something, despite it not coming easily, like when you have a strict deadline, and there's times when you shouldn't force it. You need to learn your own body and what it's trying to tell you when you're struggling to work on something. For me, it could mean my Lyme disease or Bartonella are acting up and I'm tiring myself out too much trying to draw or whatever I'm doing. It could mean I just have more brain fog or fatigue that day and my brain needs to work on something less complex.

Learn your body and know when you should force yourself to keep working on something and when you can give yourself a break and/or work on something else.

If you're struggling to figure out your work style, you probably have a mixture. That's how it is with me. Some days I work best with the music going and some days I need silence in order to concentrate. Some days I can work for 5 hours straight and some days I work in ½-hour chunks. Some days I'm all about one specific project and other days I mix it up and work on several.

There's no right or wrong way to work. You just need to figure out the right way for YOU to work, and that may be different day to day. Just try not to get lost in things that aren't moving you forward.

Don't mistake switching things up for losing focus.

When I can't focus on one thing, I move on to another thing that will still be good for my business and is connected to one of my goals.

I'm giving you permission to switch it up if you're just not making progress on something one day, but try not to jump around too much. Give yourself the time to try and focus on what you need to do and put your other life stresses aside while you do so. Your financial stresses, your life stresses, your relationship stresses… try to keep them all out of your head and out of your studio as you focus on your work. You may need to give yourself 10 minutes of meditation or silence in your studio before you begin to work. That time will allow you to decompress and clear your mind from what's stressing you out and allow you to focus on what you want to accomplish.

6
How To Create A Business Plan

Trust me when I say I know how much you're dreading this. When I started my business I didn't want to make a plan either. I dreaded it and I put it off and I put it off, refusing to do it. I figured if I had a general idea in my head, that was fine! I could work with that.

As true as that may be, having your goals (and a path to reach them) written down is the best way to go.

Finally, I applied for a Business Development Grant from the Vermont Art Council, here in my home state. In order to apply, however, I needed a fairly comprehensive business and marketing plan that I would submit to them as part of the application process.

Well, crap.

Now I really had to do it. There was no more reasoning with myself as to why it didn't matter that much or how I was better off not doing it. I no longer had a choice. If I wanted the grant, I had to make a business plan.

Around this same time I took a course called **Breaking Into Business**, which the Vermont Art Council had created for people starting their own creative businesses. It was a two-day workshop that talked about making a website, business cards, sales tax, selling online, and *making a business plan*. The teachers for this workshop provided us with a template that made the process much easier, and you can find a similar one with a simple Google search.

The main idea behind the business plan, though, was much simpler than I had initially anticipated. Instead of trying to write out every little thing I wanted to do and how I wanted to do it and the reasoning behind it and where I hoped it would get me, I mostly focused on big ideas.

When you write a business plan, think about the next year, the next 5 years, and the next 10 years and ask yourself these questions:

- What do you hope to accomplish in the next year? (Your Summit Goals!) Think of 2-5 bigger goals that you think you can do in the next 12 months.
- What are the steps you'll likely take to be able to accomplish the above? (Your Step Goals!) Think of 2-8 steps for each of the Summit Goals above.
- How much do you hope to make in Gross and in Profit in the next year? Be realistic. If you made $2000 this year, $50,000 maybe is not realistic for you, especially if you don't have any more time or energy than you did last year. But $5000 sounds reasonable. Maybe even $8,000 if you're ready to amp up your efforts and productivity and are gaining momentum with your business.
- Will anyone help you? Will you have employees, interns, assistants, volunteers, contracted workers, or other companies helping you?
- How will you measure your success or failure with your goals? (Remember, goals need to be measurable. If your goal is to make 50 paintings this year, it's easily measurable. If you're halfway there and you have only made 15 paintings, you know you're behind schedule! If your goal is to have a solo exhibit, you need to keep track of the proposals you've sent out and the responses and continue to put yourself out there. If you keep getting rejected, you might want to talk with a consultant about your proposal and if it's appealing to a gallery or

why/how it might be lacking.)

Answer all those questions for the next 12 months, and then answer them again for what you hope to accomplish in 5 years, and then again for 10 years. You can be less specific with these, as your 1-year plan is most important and what you'll be looking at to help keep you on track. Then next year, you'll do this again and see what's changed.

Don't expect to stick to everything you wrote down in your business plan.

Things change, unexpected opportunities arise, and your business will change direction in an instant. That's okay! If something you thought was going to do well is failing and not bringing in any money, move on to something that does! Wavering from your business plan is not only okay, it's expected to happen. You never know what's going to come your way, so how can you plan for it?

This is where you might be asking, then why do I have to do a plan in the first place?

That was me. Knowing plans are never a perfect road map, I used that as one of my many excuses not to create one. Why bother making a plan that's just going to change? I can't possibly plan what's going to happen because I don't know which proposals will get approved or who I'll meet, etc. etc.

Well, I wasn't wrong, but I wasn't right either.

When you sit down to create a business plan, you're collecting all of your thoughts and laying them down on paper. You're collecting your Summit Goals and pushing yourself to come up with the Step Goals that go along with them. You're thinking about the future and where you want your business to go, and what you want it to do. You're visualizing what your success would look like.

I guarantee you'll learn something about yourself and your hopes for your business during this process. Whether it's a goal you didn't realize you had, or suddenly recognizing the next steps you should take, something new will come of this that you may not have expected. Plus you may find that putting your financial goals down on paper in front of you suddenly makes them real. For example, maybe I want to make $10,000 this year, say twice as much as last year, and I'm going to attempt to do that by boosting my marketing in *this department* and reaching out to influencers in *this field* and constantly sending out proposals to *these people*, etc. Fill in your own business plan by figuring out generally where you want to go, and what you think is the best way to get there.

A business plan is just your 12-month Summit Goals, and the Step Goals you'll need to achieve them.

And if that's all it really is, there's no need to dread it. There's also no perfect formula, so if you're doing this just for yourself (not for a grant application or some other organization), then you don't even need to format it in any particular way. Just write down your bigger Summit Goals for the year with the steps to reach them listed underneath.

7
Learning To Be Efficient

A lot of people think that multitasking is the best way to accomplish things, because not only are you accomplishing one thing, you're accomplishing multiple things!

They're wrong.

Multitasking, I'm sad to say, is one of the least efficient ways to tackle your goals. I had to learn this the hard way. When I first read about this, I didn't believe it. I thought I was a masterful multitasker! I could have 7 different things going on at once and jump back and forth between them like a pro.

Through research and my own experimentation, I've come to realize that no matter how good I was at multitasking, it would never hold a candle to focusing on one project at a time and completing it, and then working on another one.

When you multitask, your brain is constantly shifting gears. It takes your brain time to go from one type of thinking to the next, so each time you switch from one to another, you lose valuable time.

If you can work on one project at a time, or at least one Step Goal at a time, and finish it before moving on to the next, you'll be a lot more productive.

Think about it this way; if you have 5 tasks that each take 8 hours to complete and you keep switching back and forth, 1 hour on this one, 2 hours on this one, 1 hour on that one, etc., you won't finish them very quickly and you'll start getting frustrated that you haven't made much progress.

Instead, if you work on one at a time, you'll finish the first one in 8 hours, the second in 16 hours, the third in 24 hours, and so on. Once you accomplish one task, you'll feel productive and it'll give you more drive to start the next one, and the next, instead of feeling bogged down constantly working on all of them.

This was a hard one for me because I naturally liked multitasking. Because of this trait I wasn't very good at finishing things. Instead, I would get about 50-75% through a project before I would lose interest. Now I entice myself to finish one thing before moving on to the next. I offer myself a reward if I finish something, or I simply say that I can't start that next new shiny idea until I finish this one. This is especially true with my artwork. I don't allow myself to start a new drawing until I finish the one I'm working on because otherwise I end up with half a dozen partially drawn pieces and never finish.

This is another place where smaller goals are important. The smaller the goal, the easier it is to accomplish and the more productive you'll feel. This tends to help with efficiency as well because you'll cruise through goal after goal and get a lot of work done.

If you're someone who can plan your time out, do that. It can make you much more efficient if you have a plan and that's your working style, like we talked about before. If it's not, that's okay, find your own working style and you'll be equally as efficient.

One great method, if you're trying to be super efficient, is to time yourself.

When I'm writing and the words aren't flowing very well, I do what are called wordsprints. All this involves is timing myself for a half hour and seeing how many words I can put to paper during that half-hour sprint. It's surprisingly effective.

Time yourself for a half hour and count how many words you wrote. Take a 5-10 minute break and time yourself for another half-hour and see how many words you wrote again.

This is especially great if you only have a couple hours to spare.

This isn't just useful for writing, either.

Working on a painting? Time yourself for a half-hour and focus as much as you can, not letting yourself be distracted by your phone, your family, or anything else. Then see how much you accomplished and take a short break. Then do it again.

This can work for a number of different tasks, whether it's writing, creating work, exercising, cleaning your studio, framing, organizing, making marketing materials, etc. If you're feeling like you need an extra boost to help motivate yourself to be efficient, take a stab at working in sprints!

Another method is to reward yourself. Maybe if you finish writing a certain number of words, you can have that cookie you've been eyeing in the kitchen. Or maybe if you sculpt for two hours, you can have that cocktail later. I tend to be food oriented, so a lot of my rewards are cookies. But maybe your reward is taking the time to have a nice long bath. Or perhaps you give yourself extra snuggle time with your loved one or your pet. Maybe it means being able to dig into that guilty pleasure book you've had on your nightstand, or baking something delicious! Whatever it is, let it motivate you to be productive and efficient now, so you can have that reward later.

I'm a positive reinforcement kind of gal, but maybe you're better when you use negative reinforcement. If you don't write 2,000 words, do you not get something? If you don't draw for two hours, are you not allowed to go out with friends? It sounds like you're punishing your high-school self, but if it helps you, do it. (Just don't start drowning yourself in guilt if you don't accomplish something because that's not helpful or necessary.)

It's like exercising. The hardest part is getting started. Then while you're doing it, try to keep yourself motivated however you can. When I was healthy I used to run almost every day. Then I'd eat ice cream. That was my reward. If I didn't run, I wasn't allowed to eat my ice cream and it kept me motivated. So did listening to music.

I typically ran five miles but if I didn't have my music I probably would have stopped at one.

Use whatever gimmick or trick or system that helps keep you motivated and working productively.

There's nothing wrong with using music to help keep you motivated. It doesn't make you any less of an artist if you need to give yourself a reward for creating. Sometimes it's hard to get started and that's okay! Just do what you can to keep moving forward, even on your down days.

And again, take breaks! Time yourself and then take a break. Complete a task and then take a break and reward yourself with a snack. Just don't reward yourself for every tiny thing. Make it for things that take you at least an hour.

Whatever helps keep you motivated, do it!

8
Handling Rejection

Rejection is something you will never be able to avoid, no matter how much you may try. And honestly, as an entrepreneur, you don't want to avoid it.

There are two common types of rejection in our lives: social rejection and professional rejection. Social rejection is when you're growing up and you want to sit at a lunch table with someone and they say no, or you ask someone out on a date and they say no. It hurts. It stings. It's humiliating.

Professional rejection is when you go for a job interview and they say no, or when you send a proposal to a gallery and they say no. It still hurts. It still stings. It can still be humiliating.

For the purpose of this book, when I say rejection I mean *professional rejection.*

Let's take a moment and define rejection. Here is the Google dictionary's take on it:

> *rejection* |*ri ˈjekSHən*|
>
> *noun*
>
> *the dismissing or refusing of a proposal, idea, etc.:* *the union decided last night to recommend rejection of the offer.*

My definition takes it a little further:

Rejection happens when what you're offering is not QUITE what the other person/company is looking for.

It's that simple. What you're offering, perhaps in a proposal for a solo exhibit, is not quite what that gallery is looking for. Perhaps they only do abstract work and yours is not abstract enough for their taste. Maybe they have had a lot of work similar to yours and therefore are booked up with that type of work.

Galleries and retailers and businesses are all looking for very specific things and it's hard to know going into a conversation with them exactly what that is. A curator may love your work and still not accept your proposal for one reason or another. This happens all the time.

As an artist, you should become very familiar with rejection. It's normal and it's good! If you're getting rejected that means you're one step ahead of the game already because you're getting your work out there! That's more than a lot of people, believe me.

If you think of my definition of rejection, it's not as bad as it initially seems. They're not necessarily saying your work is bad, it's just not right for them at that moment or in that location.

Don't let rejection stop you from continuing to send out proposals and ideas and inquiries and applications.

Be persistent. If you're getting rejected it means you haven't found the right place yet. You will if you keep looking. There are people out there who will love your work, you just need to find them. Do your research and keep searching for those perfect matches. I say matchES because I mean plural. If you finally land a solo exhibit at a gallery, congratulations! Go celebrate, but then don't be satisfied. Keep sending more proposals to more galleries until you have more successes lined up. It's a never-ending process.

Even if you get rejected, follow up.

It may seem counterintuitive to thank the person who just rejected you, but do it anyway. Make sure to follow up with the person and thank them for their time and consideration and then ask if they have any suggestions on how you could have improved your proposal, or if they have any suggestions of who else might be more interested in your type of work.

The fact that they sent you a rejection letter is great. They may have said no, but you've still made what could be a useful connection. Half the time or more you won't even get a response from a proposal or an idea you submit, so if they take the time to send you a note, that's more than most. Despite their rejection, try to nurture that new connection to see if there's any future to it. Do they know anyone who might like your work? Do they have suggestions? Would they be open to you resubmitting in the future? Are there events coming up where you might be able to meet them in person?

A "no" doesn't mean someone hates you, despite how it may feel. *No just means you weren't quite what they were looking for at the moment.*

Lastly, move on quickly. Let's face it, you don't have the time or energy to spend wallowing about being rejected. You've got stuff to do! So read the letter during one of your email/correspondence check-in times of the day, write a BRIEF letter back, showing gratitude and graciousness, and then MOVE ON. Don't even give it another thought, just put it in the file of no's and get back to work on something that might turn into a yes.

You can't avoid rejection, not if you're putting yourself out there like you should be to grow your business. But you can learn from it. If someone who rejects you writes back when you ask them if they have suggestions, take those notes to heart. Some may make sense to implement into your future proposals, and some may not resonate with you.

Avoid having the knee-jerk reaction of being angry at the person for saying no. Saying no sucks too. I have to say no all the time and I hate it. Gallery owners and retailers and other professionals you will be reaching out to probably say no a lot more than I do, and I can almost guarantee they don't like it either.

Just because someone rejects you doesn't mean they're mean, it doesn't mean they have horrible taste, it doesn't mean they're dumb, or anything else. It just means *what you were offering wasn't quite right for them!* Remember?

If you keep putting yourself out there and reaching out to people, even if you keep getting rejected, you're learning from your mistakes, you're making some possibly great connections. One of these days when you might be expecting another rejection there will be an acceptance instead!

9
Legal And Bookwork

Even when you're just starting a business, you have to pay attention to the legalities of it, including keeping track of your bookkeeping. This is a short chapter but I wanted to make it a chapter of its own to draw attention to it.

Proper bookkeeping and legal requirements are important!

This part of running a business may not be your forte. It's certainly not mine. I hate it. I dread it more than anything. But I make sure to do it and do it correctly. This is one of those aspects of business where I have absolutely no motivation, so I definitely get cookies when I finish it. So many cookies. Maybe even a brownie or ice cream.

Learn it.

Don't hope you know what you're doing and pray for the best. Do actual research, talk to an actual lawyer and accountant (they have some that help artists for free or very cheap), and learn how to do it all properly.

- Do you need insurance? What type(s)?
- Are you registered as a business? Should you trademark your business name?
- What about copyrights?

- Are you an LLC, a sole proprietor, or a corporation? What's the differences between those and how would they apply to your particular business?
- Are you keeping track of all your expenses and keeping receipts?
- Do you know how to file your taxes for your business as an entrepreneur?
- Are you keeping a spreadsheet with details about your expenses and your income (profit/loss)?
- Are you signed up and paying your sales tax either monthly or quarterly? Do you need to pay other taxes?
- And even smaller things like: If you make a YouTube video, is your music and all your imaging credited and you're certain you can use them royalty free?
- Or if you use reference photos from others for your artwork, do you have written permission from the photographer to use them?
- How about if you do commissions? Do you have a contract written up that your client signs before you begin? What should that contract say?
- And so on…

Don't procrastinate.

Yes, bookwork and legal stuff can all be boring and monotonous and confusing. It can be overwhelming, especially in the beginning when you're just learning the processes. So take it a little at a time. Create STEP GOALS. Chip at it in little chunks until you understand and can get it all done.

Procrastinating on things like this will just make you dread it more and then it will be hanging over your head and you'll feel guilty for not doing it and it will weigh on you. Do it, get it done, and move on. You'll thank yourself later.

Get help from professionals if you need it.

Don't shy away from asking for help with this type of stuff, or anything for that matter. It's the phrase, "there's no need to reinvent the wheel" at work here. People everywhere do this all the time, so ask them for help. You can ask me for help, ask a lawyer for help, ask an accountant for help, ask your parents, siblings, friends, and colleagues for help. Whoever might have the best input for whatever situation you're in. If there's a business consultant nearby, or a business clinic, or a group of entrepreneurs that gets together monthly, go seek them out. If you can make connections while also learning useful information, that's always a win-win.

10
Do Your Research

Research can be tricky. You certainly want to do your research, and about many different things. When you're first starting out, a lot of your research should be market research. Research things like:

- Who's your target market or ideal customer?
- Who are the big players and influencers in your field?
- How are those people marketing themselves?
- Where/how do your ideal customers shop? Is online better or worse than in person?
- Are there places near you where your ideal customers might shop and are they accepting proposals for new work?

Once you get some of your initial research done and you know who your audience is likely to be, you might start researching things like:

- How to build your business
- Co-marketing
- Branding
- Helpful software, email servers, website hosts, website developers

- Growing your business
- Selling online
- Craft shows
- Art marketing + workshops
- Blogging
- Reproductions and products made of your artwork or craft
- And so on…

This is all great and you should definitely be doing this type of research, and the fact that you're reading this book on how to build your art business means you're already one step ahead! Go you!

But researching can be surprisingly tricky. Here's some things to remember as you're doing research:

Use quality sources. Not everyone's opinion on the internet is going to be valid or helpful to your situation. Read about the writer for any blog post or article or book that you're about to read to see where they're coming from and what experience they have before trusting their opinion.

Research where you think you're lacking. If you're great at blogging, you probably don't need to spend as much time researching that as you should researching aspects of your business you're not so great at. If you think you're lacking in an area, research it! There's loads of information on the internet and it's all a quick Google search away. Take advantage.

Don't let it be a time waste. Research can easily turn into a time waster and a way to procrastinate, as you probably well know. In the beginning I found myself researching how to build my business and I would go from one article to the next to the next, gaining all this information but never implementing much of it because I was wasting all my time reading about it. Don't let your precious time get chewed up by your research.

Maybe you should make one day a week be your research day. Or perhaps one hour each morning, or two hours once a week. Whatever you do, don't get so distracted by learning about everything that you don't implement what you've learned.

Implement what you learn, but not all at once. It's great to continuously research and learn and keep up to date on things relating to your field, your audience, and building your business. That's actually a goal you should have as an entrepreneur. But make sure you're not just reading in order to read. Prioritize your research to be things you can actually use in your own business and try not to read articles that have no use or are unrelated to you.

The other problem is over-implementing what you learn. Don't get so caught up in learning a bunch of new things that you feel like you have to go and implement them all at once. Keep your goals in sight and focus on whichever new idea will get you closest to that goal the quickest. Implement that, see how it goes, and THEN think about some of the other ideas your research has fostered.

Don't let new ideas overwhelm you. Just because you research something doesn't mean you have to do it. If a well-known artist is blogging about how well they're doing selling their work at craft shows and how that's the only way they make any real money, don't think it will automatically be the same for you. If you despise doing craft shows, then don't do them. There are plenty of other ways you can build your business, and certainly ones that are less physically intensive.

Thinking you have to be just like someone else who seems successful in your area, or believing you need to do one specific thing to be successful, are both false.

You also don't need to do EVERYTHING. I'll talk about this more later, but I'll mention it now too. When it comes to marketing, social media has a large role to play. But that doesn't mean you have to be on every social media platform out there. If you're most comfortable with Facebook, then focus on that one. If you're going to do them, do them well and post consistently. You don't have to do it all.

It's the same with any sort of marketing. If you're getting told over and over again that you absolutely need a blog but you hate writing and are horrible about being consistent when it comes to that and you'll dread every minute of it, which will also make it take up more of your precious time, then don't do it. You can always add it later if you change your mind, but for right now you don't have to do it.

Focus on the things and actions you know work for you, and do them well. Don't let those fantastic new ideas you've been researching distract you from your business goals. You already know what you want out of your business from your business plan and goals. Now you're just using your research to help you get there more quickly and more professionally.

11
Know Your Limits

Keep in mind this is coming from someone with a chronic illness, but I think it's incredibly important, whether you're sick or healthy, to know your limits. It can be difficult to assess when you can push yourself and when to pull back. This is especially true for anyone in a similar position to me where I have good days and bad days because of my illnesses. Sometimes a good day can turn into a bad day because I push too hard to get something done and then I regret it.

It's not always easy to know when to push, when to pull back, but try to listen to your body. If you're body or brain is screaming at you to slow down and take a break, do it. You'll regret it if you don't. Even strict deadlines should take a backseat to your own physical and mental health.

You're no use to anyone if you're too stressed out to function properly.

If you have a cold or the flu, take it a little easier. You may have a deadline or be frustrated you're not getting more done, but the more you rest, the more you can let your body work on fighting whatever is attacking your system, and the faster you'll likely get over it. Drink fluids and rest. Maybe find a way where you can work on the couch or in a recliner on a project, so you're not using as much energy. Do whatever you need to do in order to lessen the stress on your body.

Take it from someone who knows, your health is the most important priority. Never let your job or your side hustle take over your health, your sanity, or your relationships with those you love. Those things need to ALWAYS come first, no matter what.

I'm not saying that sometimes your work doesn't take you away from your family, or that if you have a cold you shouldn't do anything at all. What I'm saying is that it shouldn't always come first. Don't let your work take priority over everything else. Work to live, don't live to work. If your body is in some serious need of a break, take it. Don't feel guilty for putting your own needs first and wanting to maintain a healthy relationship with your spouse and kids.

Trying to find a balance is always a struggle. You can do it. It may not always feel like it, and you might start to wobble off course, but if you can recognize that it's starting to overwhelm your life, then you can put actions into place that move you back on track.

This means sometimes you're going to have to say no. Learning to say no is a difficult task, especially if it's something you actually do want to do, but you know you don't currently have the time or energy to do it. Again, it's a balancing act. You need to be realistic with yourself when deciding which projects to pursue and which ones to skip.

Prioritize the projects that will move you forward.

If you're offered a huge opportunity that you think you're capable of accomplishing and doing well, one that will move your business forward in a big way, then take it! Make room for it in your schedule and make it a new goal and priority. Just don't let it push aside anything that is more important for your business.

If you're offered an opportunity that sounds like a fun idea, but you're only getting paid in "exposure" for days or weeks worth of your time, and you're not sure if that exposure will bring in any new sales or clients, then think twice before agreeing to do it.

Artists deserve to be paid with a whole lot more than "Good Exposure."

"Good exposure" is a ridiculous expectation that has cropped up in the creative industry, and my personal opinion is that artists should not accept it. It belittles your time and energy. If it were any other industry, you'd be getting paid for your time and materials fairly. "Good exposure" might mean great things will happen, of course, or it might mean nothing. I've had projects and exhibits with great exposure that didn't bring in a single new client. I've had some with limited exposure that brought in multiple new clients. You never know what exposure might mean.

Therefore, exposure should be an added benefit of a project, not the basis of your pay. You work hard and your time is valuable. Charge them for it. People get what they pay for and the only reason "good exposure" is still acceptable to some in this industry is because artists are buying into that myth.

Recognize your value and expect that clients will respect your time. If they don't, move on.

A lot of public art clients don't realize what they're asking for is inconsiderate. Unless you're an artist or you know artists well, you may not realize how much energy and time and focus goes into creating something. I know plenty of people who thought they were doing me a huge favor by offering me a job with "good exposure," but what they didn't realize was I don't have the time or energy to spend on things that don't pay me and I KNOW will move my business forward.

That's why we need to teach them. Politely.

If someone tells you they have a great project for you that you know will take a lot of time and all they're offering is "good exposure," think twice about accepting and then tell them why you're hesitating or turning them down. Let them know that you're so flattered they thought of you for this project and that they like your work, but you estimate it will take *this* number of hours to complete, and materials are expected to cost *this* much. So if you were to take on a project like that, as a professional artist with a lot already going on, you'd have to be guaranteed to make at least *this* amount. Explain to them that you have a lot on your plate, things that are paying jobs, and you don't have the time to take on anything that doesn't pay you, but again, thanks so much for thinking of you. If there is any way the person could get sponsors to cover your estimated expenses and time, then that would be great! Otherwise, unfortunately you must decline the request.

There's nothing wrong with saying no, despite how difficult it can be. It can make you feel guilty or inconsiderate, especially because you know how bad rejection can feel! But you need to push those feeling aside.

Remember, you're running a business. You don't have the time to spend on things that aren't actively building that business!

If you are in a position where you feel you should say no, just make sure to do it politely and when possible, explain why. "I'm sorry, but I have a lot going on right now and I can only take on projects that will pay me *this* much an hour to cover my time and expenses. Thanks so much for thinking of me for this project! I'm so glad you like my work. If you have future projects where I might be a better fit, don't hesitate to reach out…."

People will respect you if you're professional, and it will add to your credibility. Be as honest and open as possible. It doesn't mean others might not still get mad at you sometimes or become inconsiderate themselves, but that's their problem. If they're not professional enough to recognize that rejection in this polite form is just the fact that *what they're offering isn't QUITE what you're looking for*, and they become mean or belligerent, then they're not worth your time or energy and you should be even more thankful you said no.

Likewise, don't ever take time to engage people who are negative to you for no reason.

If someone comes over to you and starts saying degrading things about you or your artwork, ie. "My 5-year-old could make better art than that," or "What's your REAL job?" or "People actually like this type of artwork?" or any number of other insults, don't engage. Be as polite and professional as you can be because your reputation is at stake, it's just not worth the energy to argue with anyone.

If you post a video online and trolls are everywhere tearing you and your video down, ignore it or report them. Don't spend time reading all the negative comments or getting caught up in what they say. Move on and keep working toward your goals.

There's a lot of mean people online nowadays and they're just waiting for new material to appear on the web for them to write nasty comments about. That's not your problem, that's theirs. And if you have good content you're putting out there, lots of times your own audience will fight back for you and you shouldn't get involved at all.

The only time you should get involved is if it's a customer support issue and someone's not happy with a product in a review. In this instance you should write a polite message back to them, such as, "Hi *name*. I'm so sorry to hear you weren't satisfied with your order! We're more than willing to offer you a full refund (or credit on your website, or some other bonus) to help fix this issue. Is that something that would be of interest to you? If you have any questions or further concerns, please feel free to contact us! (with link to your contact page or email address)"

This isn't necessarily the same as engaging with online trolls, this could be a legitimate disappointed customer, and as we all know, word of mouth is hugely important in a business, so you don't want anyone to be disappointed and then tell their friends and family about it.

Aim to have the best customer service imaginable.

Sometimes this will take away from your projects and it's annoying and frustrating, but this is important and you need to take the time to do it. A lot of my customers right now are RETURN customers, and for this very reason. So as much as you want to avoid the black hole of negative commenters and people, this is different and deserves your time and energy.

Keep in mind you only have so much energy to go around, and only so much time to get everything done. If you plan things out well, either on paper or in your head, hopefully you won't feel like you're rushing yourself through tasks. Then you can spend the appropriate amount of time on each one.

Don't overbook yourself.

You're only one person, you can only do so much. If you are taking on more projects and clients than you can handle, you're getting overly stressed, you're overwhelmed with everything you have to do, and you're exhausted… it sounds to me like you're not respecting your limits.

Every business has an ebb and flow, peaks and valleys. There will be months when you're wondering how you're going to get everything done and clients are popping up all over the place, and then there are months when you're wondering where the heck all those clients went and why some of them aren't showing up now, when you have more time?

Things can get crazy and you may not have much control over that. But you do have control over how you handle it and if you're saying yes to everything or if you're appropriately prioritizing which projects you should do and which ones you should skip for now.

One thing about having limited time or limited energy is recognizing that you may not be physically capable of growing your business as quickly as you'd like.

If you're running this business by yourself and you only have weekends to work on it, then you might not be able to grow to a $100,000 business in the first few years. That's probably not be reasonable, unless of course you want to quit your day job and work on it full-time. Even then, that's a lofty goal for that time limit.

Building a business takes energy and drive, and if you're lacking in one of those areas, like I am due to my chronic illnesses, then you have to realize that if you want to grow your business, you have to be especially smart about it.

I can't do many craft shows, they're just too exhausting. I know that, so despite a lot of invitations to do them, I tend to say no. Of course, I could hire someone to go do them for me, but at this point I've not seen enough revenue from the ones I've done to make that a smart business idea. Instead, I focus on exhibits and passive income.

I know I don't have as much energy as the average person and that my energy is also inconsistent. Therefore, I plan out my business in a way that makes sense for my own limitations. I make products from my artwork that I sell on my website, like reproductions, greeting cards, mousepads, and others that don't require a ton of work for me to be able to fill an order. I create digital products, like YouTube video tutorials, downloadable PDFs, and ebooks, where I don't have to use any energy at all when someone orders them (after the initial energy of making them).

These types of purposeful actions in my business are what allow me to grow it while still not pushing myself past the brink of sanity and harming my already fragile health. So when it comes to your own business, look carefully at your limitations and what's causing them. You need to objectively analyze your situation and decide how quickly you could feasibly grow your business (remember, as it grows you can always hire people to help you out too). You need to decide if the products or services you're selling are the best ones for your growth, or if they'll cause you to be overwhelmed when business picks up.

Let's look at a couple examples. I get asked to do commissions all the time. Commissions are great because they give you a chunk of money, you get good word of mouth (hopefully) from your clients, and if it's in your contract, you may be able to use the final image for other products and make even more money off of them. But I know I can only do a certain number of commissions before they take up all of my time.

Don't get me wrong, some artists can make a killing doing commissions as the main aspect of their business, but just know that it automatically limits your growth. If a commission takes you an average of 20 hours to do, and you work 20 hours a week, even if that's ALL you do (which it shouldn't be because you should also be marketing in order to get more clients!), you could do 1 commission a week. If you work EVERY week without a break, also something shouldn't do if you don't want to get worn out, you can do 52 commissions in a year, at the absolute maximum. This example obviously doesn't take into account anything potentially going wrong, variations in the amount of time on each one, etc.

If you're doing each commission for $1000, which is being generous, then you just made $52,000 a year with commissions. That's certainly nothing to snuff at!

HOWEVER, that's the top amount you could ever earn that way and you have no time to do your own creative work or take a break or work on marketing.

Unless suddenly you can work full-time and then you can double it. Boom, you're now making $104,000, and probably completely burnt out and hating your job. But that's a great chunk of change. Is it worth it? Maybe it is for you, but if you're reading this book, I'm thinking you're ready to learn ways in which you can grow more easily, with less of your time being gobbled up by one activity.

Again, know your limits. I don't particularly like doing commissions, and I have a lot of other things I work on, so I only accept a few commissions a year. Plus my artwork takes longer than most, averaging 40-100 hours per piece, so it's a huge time suck.

I already know my limits and that in order to grow I need passive income, so commissions are limited for that reason. They're just too energy-intensive to be a sustainable way for me to do business, and the growth is limited to how many I can do.

If I sell prints of my artwork, on the other hand, I am unlimited in how many I can do. Prints aren't a one-time thing, so even though they may bring in less money than a commission on an individual basis, I can sell more and more and it doesn't take up nearly as much of my time. I can order any number of prints at once, unlike having to draw each commission out by hand. It takes a little energy because I have to have a good scan of the drawing (a one-time energy task), and call or go online to order the prints, but it can grow exponentially without becoming overwhelming for me. And the more I sell, the easier it is to hire someone to help me out with that facet of my business, whereas with commissions I have to do them all myself and I can't hire someone to share the workload.

Let's recap because this was a long chapter.

Know your limits:
- Always put your health, sanity, and relationships first.
- Learn when you can push yourself and when you should pull back and let yourself rest. Listen to your body.
- Learn to say no and prioritize the projects that make the most sense for you and your business.
- Give yourself enough time to do everything without getting overwhelmed and stressed.
- Be completely open and honest with everyone about what limitations you may have.
- Don't take on projects that are beyond what you have the time or energy to do.
- Know how much and how quickly you can realistically grow your business.
- Prioritize your products and services based on how well you can grow your business with them, keeping in mind how your limitations play into each, ie: Commissions vs. Reproductions vs. Teaching Workshops vs. Craft Fairs vs. Digital Products, etc.

12
Deadlines

This chapter is short and goes into a little more detail about something I mentioned in the last one. Deadlines.

Can you work on a deadline? I very rarely do. In my short client contract there's actually a line that says I will not work on a deadline. The project may get done quickly, or it may take a while and my clients need to be okay with that from the get-go.

The reason I started adding this part in was because of my chronic illness. I never know how I'm going to feel or if unforeseen circumstances will keep me from drawing for a week, a month, or multiple months at a time. Therefore, I don't guarantee any sort of timeline. I'm upfront with my client and explain the situation and so far everyone has been great at being patient and understanding.

That being said, if I were to be 100% healthy starting tomorrow, this is still something I would implement. It's not a way for me to be lazy and not work at a productive pace. On the contrary, I usually get things done sooner than people expect. But I'm well aware of life throwing curveballs and I don't want to commit myself to having something done in two weeks and then come down with a horrible flu or have a family member be sick and in the hospital and I have to worry about a deadline on top of this other sudden stress. Instead I can contact my client with a brief update that something has come up and it'll likely take a little longer than I expected, but because I have that statement in my contract and have discussed it with them in the beginning, I'm not worried about it.

The very rare times I do allow a client to put me on a deadline, say for a poster design that needs to be ready to go to print by a certain date, or for a publication, or in order to fulfill the timeline for a grant, I make sure I do one thing:

Leave myself plenty of time and wiggle room.

Think realistically. If you're estimating it'll take you about 40 hours to do a project for someone, and you're working full-time, you might be tempted to say you can do it in a week! Don't do that. Never do that.

Instead, leave yourself time to do other things that need to be done too. Do you write a weekly blog? Add that time in. What about filling orders? Correspondence? Marketing? Your other step goals? Add time in for those too, limiting them because the deadline is your priority.

Then add wiggle room.

Let's say with all the other stuff you should also be doing in that time, it's now a two-week project. When you add wiggle room, in case something happens, now it's a three-week project and some of the stress of that deadline has decreased.

Sometimes you can negotiate a timeline with your client, and other times it's already fixed, so it's your job to make sure you're leaving yourself enough time and that you're not committing to something you can't accomplish.

Again, be upfront and honest with your client from the beginning. Don't jump to say you can do something in a certain amount of time without thinking it through first.

Another thing to keep in mind is that you don't always have to work on someone else's schedule.

Your time is equally as important as someone else's, so you don't always have to fall in line with THEIR schedule.

If you're partnering with another business and they say they need something done in a week and haven't given you much notice, then they may not be respecting your time. If that schedule doesn't work for you because you have other commitments, then politely let them know how much time this project is going to take for you and that you already have prior commitments that need to come first. Then tell them you'll likely be able to get it done in two weeks, or however long you need (with a little wiggle room!) and see if that will still work for them.

Keep in mind you're running your own business here. Nobody is your boss but you.

If someone is being belligerent or inconsiderate or dismissive of your needs, don't waste your time. If you've signed a contract, either try to get out of it or finish it out and don't work with them again. You already have a large amount of stress just from trying to run and build your own business, you don't need stress thrown on from other people too. It's not worth it. Remember to put your own sanity and wellbeing first and foremost.

I give you permission to say no!

If you feel that working on deadlines is not for you, there's nothing wrong with that. That's what I do and I still typically get a finished product to my client before they expect it. It's the same as that smart business quote: **under-promise and over-deliver**. If you tell people it might take 1-2 weeks to ship an item and they get it in 5 days, they're going to be a very happy customer. Plus it gives you wiggle room in case something goes wrong and it actually does take two weeks once in a while.

13
Learning To Adapt

When people ask me what the number one thing that leads to success is, I usually say persistence and adaptation. Persistence is key to getting yourself in the door for many places. If you don't follow up and keep putting yourself out there over and over again despite being rejected, you'll never succeed.

You can't let rejection or failures slow you down. Keep moving forward.

When it comes to adaptation, it's a little different. Adaptation is necessary because things will not go the way you expect. You might have the greatest and most descriptive business plan on the planet, but within a few weeks or months, something will go wrong. Something you expected to be a huge seller will flop, something else might take off, and nothing is quite fitting that extraordinary plan you laid out.

Don't worry about it.

Just because things aren't going according to your plan, doesn't mean your business isn't still moving forward and growing.

For example, this year I did a quick business plan and laid out my Summit Goals on one of my whiteboards during the first week of January. I was on top of it! I had everything laid out and

Summit Goals prioritized and a general idea of how this year was going to go, if things went well.

Well, a week later I was asked to participate in an exhibit that supported a charity where each artist gets a wooden heart to decorate. These pieces were going to be auctioned off, starting at $75 each (they're pretty small), and go up from there. Half of the proceeds would go to the charity, which was one I have supported in the past, Spectrum – Youth & Family Services out of Burlington, VT. They do great work and since some of the proceeds were still coming to me, I said yes.

So I picked up my little wooden heart and stared at it. Would my preferred medium, colored pencil, work on this wooden template? Should I cut a piece of heavyweight drawing paper and cover it first? I'd never tried drawing on wood before.

I decided to try it and start drawing the kitten I had in mind directly on the wood. If it didn't work, I'd just cover it with my drawing paper and start it again.

Turns out, it worked great. So great that the next week I went all around town trying to find different types of wood to experiment with and draw on and proceeded to do more drawings on different shaped wooden plaques.

This spurred the idea that I could also decorate unfinished furniture. I'm a 2D artist, so when I do a solo exhibit I always feel like it's missing that 3D aspect to the exhibit. If I did a few tables, stools, and benches with my artwork on them, that would add a great 3D aspect to my exhibits and also give people another option to buy my artwork on a functional item.

All of this happened within January and suddenly I was applying for two grants to help me buy materials in order to make this idea come true. Was this anywhere in my business plan I'd made two weeks earlier? Not even close! I had no idea this would happen, but I'm loving it and having a ball, while also expanding my business in a way I didn't expect, and as I keep doing it I'll measure how my audience receives it and whether or not it's worth pursuing and optimizing.

This type of project is similar to commissions, in that I can only make so many each year. So I plan to limit how many I do as originals and then partner with someone who can make the same piece of furniture with a printed reproduction of the original. Then I can sell reproductions that will take less time to produce. If it takes off, I can hire someone to help or take the reproduction part of the business over.

As you can see, one of my biggest goals for the year popped up out of nowhere. It was a surprise and I jumped at the opportunity despite not having planned for it at all. Some of my other goals have already fallen to the back burner as my health has been an issue, and others I'm progressing on well. That's just how it works.

As things change, adapting quickly is key to success.

If you can't see the writing on the wall, so to speak, and adapt when things aren't working out or when something surprising happens, then you're not likely to be successful. You need to be able to go with the flow.

In order to adapt, you need to keep researching and keep your eyes open for things that might work better than what you're already doing, or what might supplement part of your business that's not doing well right now, or in order to promote something more that's doing surprisingly well.

Ask yourself things like:

- Is your audience craving something a little different? (Ask them.)
- Are you serving the audience you really think you are? (Is your target customer the type of person you think they are, or are your sales showing someone else buying more of your work?)
- Would a different service or product be better?
- Can you modify your current product or service to better serve your market?
- Would blogging help drive traffic?
- Should you advertise? If so, where?

Sometimes something even more frustrating happens; you have a product or service that is selling well for a while and your business may be heavily focused on that, and then it peeters out and sales drop.

Sometimes there's no way to avoid having your bestselling item suddenly drop and become less popular. Sometimes you can.

If it comes down to your customer service for repeat customers, or advertising in the right ways to keep getting new customers, you can help control that. But if the market suddenly changes and one of your top products is an innocent victim of that change, there's not much you can do about it.

This happens. Sometimes your commissions will be doing well, so you're focusing most your energy on those, and then suddenly you can't find a client for two months and you're left wondering what to do.

This is when adapting is especially important, and so is having multiple streams of income.

14
Why You Need Multiple Streams Of Income

The best way to make sure you don't fall into the trap mentioned in the last chapter, of having a bestselling item or service suddenly dry up and have most of your income drop, is to have multiple streams of income.

Multiple streams of income allow you to have a more predictable flow of income because it doesn't rely on one specific product or service.

For example if you're a painter, you can sell original paintings, reproductions, products made from your paintings, you can teach workshops, create online courses, create other digital products, etc.

Maybe you're a muralist. Your main job is creating murals in public spaces, which relies on you creating each piece. This limits what you can make for an income, but if you can also teach workshops about mural painting, write an ebook about mural painting, create downloadable tutorials about different materials you can use for murals and how to go about getting mural clients, etc., then you're creating multiple streams of income.

It's great if you have a bestselling item. That's fantastic that so many people have connected with that one product where they're willing to part with their hard-earned money to have it. That's the goal, right? But if you only have ONE thing that is selling well and you don't have a backup in case that suddenly changes, that's not good. I'm not saying ignore your bestseller. If anything, amp up the exposure of that piece because it's obviously very popular! Just keep working on other things that can bring in income as well that are unrelated to that particular piece. That way you're better off now, and more prepared in case something changes.

Here's some other ways you might be able to create multiple streams of income with your artwork or craft:

- **Licensing**. Ever thought about licensing your artwork? Companies are looking for designs for their apparel and products all the time. Do some research and see if licensing your work might be for you! Would it look great on t-shirts? On mugs? On scarves? Check out companies that might be interested in using your artwork for this type of product and what they're willing to pay you in royalties.

- **Book Illustration.** If you're a 2D artist, maybe you would be interested in illustration? Painters, illustrators, and mixed media artists alike have taken their talents and pushed them out into the publishing world. Children's books especially need artists, or you can create your own children's book! Or how about textbooks? Is your artwork intricate and detailed and you have a knack for science? Anatomy books, biology books, and many others need illustrators. Again, do the necessary research and see if this fits you.

- **Graphic Design.** Good on a computer? Maybe a part-time gig doing freelance graphic design is for you! You can choose the projects you're interested in and which clients you want to work with, as long as you're freelancing and working for yourself. Or you could work part-time for a company, but you'll have a lot less flexibility in your schedule and what you're working on. But if you're great at branding and working in programs like Photoshop and Illustrator, then maybe this is the perfect fit for you as another stream of income. Just remember, unless you're really into graphic design and it's an integral part of your art business, this may not push the rest of your art business forward. Instead, there's the possibility it will overtake it and suddenly you are working primarily on graphic design and not your own artwork. So keep that in mind.

- **Teaching.** This is something a lot of artists gravitate toward, and there's a reason! It can pay well and feel great to impart your knowledge on a class that's hungry to learn. Whether it's adult workshops or working with kids, this can be a fun and fulfilling path that also gives you another source of income. The downfall with this track is that it's time intensive. You have to actually be there to teach the workshop. It means you can't be very flexible with your schedule, you need to either partner with an organization that does workshops or hold them in your own home, or rent a space to hold them, and you have to like teaching. If you don't like it, don't do it. You may even need to make an investment before the workshop to buy materials for everyone and possibly rent a space. You should also invest in a little advertising, unless you already have a group of students who will be there. You need to decide how much to charge, how many students you can accommodate, what materials they'll need, how long the workshop is, etc. For all these reasons, I don't do many workshops, as they take too much time and energy, similar to craft shows.

- **Tutorials and Downloadable Products.** I'm a fan of things your customers can download because that's passive income and there's an unlimited supply of your product. It takes energy from you to create the product, but then you can upload it to your website or Etsy or somewhere else online and you can invest very little energy in it after that, other than promotion. This includes video tutorials, PDF tutorials, online courses, ebooks, art wallpapers, etc.

- **Write.** Are you good at writing? Do you have a blog? If so, have you monetized your blog with affiliate links, or advertising, or at least mentioning your products in your posts? Or, how about books and ebooks? Know a good deal of useful information having to do with your artwork or some aspect of your business? Maybe writing a book is a good idea for you.

- **Wholesale.** Yes, artists are able to wholesale, and it can be incredibly lucrative. Not sure because you make one-of-a-kind work? There are lots of success stories with artists who have done just that. Maybe you're a potter and your work would do well in stores that specialize in home goods or kitchen supplies? How about selling prints of your wildlife artwork to zoos and aquarium gift shops? Maybe your handmade furniture is perfect for a small furniture chain nearby? Or perhaps your jewelry would work great at a big chain store, or a local shop. There's lots to consider here, and which way you go depends on your products. I suggest starting with a few local places to get the hang of working with retailers and as a wholesaler yourself, and then move to regional places and possibly national chains. There's also wholesale shows like the **Best In American Made** where creative people show their wares and retailers come to check them out and scoop up some new wholesale clients.

- **Online Courses.** If you like to teach but you don't have the time or you can't guarantee that you'll be somewhere at a designated time, then maybe creating an online course is for you! This way you can create it a little at a time and it doesn't have to be all at once or on any kind of schedule. When you're finished you just upload it and it's a digital product people can buy and download or buy and go back to whenever they want. You can do this on your own website if you have a good following, or you can tap into the audience other websites already have, like Udemy, Teachable, Craftsy, and more. Research the different types of learning websites for this type of online course, what their specifications are, and if your course would be a good fit. The only problem with this stream of income is production. You need to have a way to film a good quality video, with good quality audio as well, and some basic video editing ability.

- **Sell Online Via A Third Party.** Ever heard of Fine Art America? How about Redbubble? These are sites where you can upload your artwork and they create products like pillows, prints, mugs, clothing, etc. with your artwork and you get a cut of whatever sells. These sites are very large and have a lot of competition. If you're able to promote it and work at it, they could be very good for you, but I haven't found them to do much for me. But then again, I heavily promote my own website where I get all the proceeds instead of those sites where I get very little. For example, you might only get $3 if you sell a pillow with your artwork on it, which is a $25 sale.
- **Etsy, Amazon Handmade, Ebay.** Etsy, Amazon Handmade, and Ebay are a little different. These are third party sites, but you do all the work and you get most of the profit. These are more like a platform for selling your work. These are also enormous, so you get the benefit of having a huge audience shopping on them, but there's also a huge amount of competition. Each one has its little quirks, so do your research before starting

to upload listings. What's important here is to use good keywords so that people can find your products easily in the search. Also, great product photos. Great photos should be used for EVERYTHING, but especially in this type of atmosphere so they stand out and you look professional. Good, clear, bright photos immediately add to your credibility as a professional with quality work.

- **And more…** There's plenty of other ways to create multiple streams of income. Do the research and find what works best for your business, your style, and your own limitations or time restraints.

The more parts of your business you add, the more time and energy it's going to take. Choose wisely. Don't spread yourself too thin, especially if you're dealing with energy problems or time restraints already. Prioritize your projects and stay on the lookout for things that will enhance your business without overwhelming you or causing too much stress. You don't have to do everything. Choose what works for you.

15
Creating A Community

There's a reason artists can sometimes be thought of as socially awkward or hermits. It's true, a lot of the time we're locked up in our studios by ourselves, working on our latest piece of artwork. We're in our own worlds. We don't necessarily have coworkers. We don't have a boss or colleagues. Our days are spent by ourselves, getting work done.

Because of that, being an artist can be lonely. It's no wonder we struggle with our own self-esteem and have to bat down the voices inside our heads that constantly doubt our abilities. When you're alone, pouring your soul into your artwork, it can be amazing, but it also fosters a social anxiety that makes us think we're not good enough. Not to mention, it means you're going about your business all alone and not getting input and advice and resources you could get from other people.

Creating a supportive community is one of the most important parts of success.

You've probably heard the saying, it's not what you know, it's WHO you know. Well, that can ring true in a lot of ways. Making connections within your field is always a good approach to advancing your business. If you go to a conference and meet the head of a big art blog and they like you and your work, they may then feature you on their website and you just gained access to a much larger audience than you previously had. Plus if you nurture that relationship, they may be willing and able to help you out in the future with something else.

On a smaller scale, let's say you're getting into the market of creating reproductions of your work, but you're having a terrible time figuring out which company and type of print you should use. You're researching and just getting more confused about which papers, which companies, which ink types and everything else. Should you stay local or go with a company that's national? Which type of finish? Canvas or paper prints? How about metal? It can be a confusing process, but there are artists all over the place who have already maneuvered their way through that maze. If you go to community events and meet some of them, or go to a reception of someone whose work you like and they have beautiful prints for sale, ask them questions! I get asked where I get my prints done all the time and I'm more than happy to recommend my print company (American Art Editions, based out of North Carolina, if you're wondering), because I am very satisfied with them and I know it can be hard to find a professional, good quality printer for these products.

Benefits of getting out and networking with other artists:

- **Share knowledge.** Learning a new technique and want to talk to someone about how it's not going quite the way you hoped? You might meet the perfect person if you get out and network within your community. Looking for the best varnish for your type of work? Someone near you might know!

- **Share Resources.** When it comes to printing, framing, and selling your work, there's a lot of information out there. What are the best resources? When you meet up with a group of other local artists, information like this starts flowing. Where's the best local frame shop? Print shop? Where is everyone else selling their work? What's the best platform for a website? Best place to buy art materials? A good place to find coupons? How about calls to artists? Get the scoop by networking with people who are friendly and like-minded.

- **Don't Feel So Isolated.** It's fine to spend the majority of your time locked in your studio, but don't forget to get out and socialize. Not only is it good for your own well-being to get out and talk to people, it will help you gain new perspectives, get feedback on your artwork, and realize that other people are going through the exact same thing you are. You're not alone! And when you're talking with your new artist friends, you might just have a sudden epiphany that leads to a new and useful idea for your business.

- **Meet Awesome People.** Let's face it, artists are cool. Some of the most interesting, weird, crazy, creative, happy, funny, and down to earth people I've ever met have been artists. There's something about us that makes us stand out from the crowd and live our life our own way. Our brains work differently, which is why artists seem so mysterious and interesting to the rest of the world. Like Queen Victoria said, *"Beware of artists. They mix with all classes of society and are therefore most dangerous."*

- **Grow Your Audience.** Ever think about collaborating? Maybe you should. Not only will it take you outside your comfort zone, it'll open you up to a new audience, essentially that of whomever your partnering with. Maybe you're at a gathering at a local gallery or event and you start talking with someone and they reveal to you that they're the curator for a gallery you like and gee, they really like your work. You may have just opened yourself up to a gallery exhibit just by showing up to that event.

Nowadays, community isn't just in person. Your online community could prove just as useful and as full of opportunities as that of your local community. If you're interested in social media, that's great. Facebook is especially useful for joining groups that are specific to anything you're looking for, and the artists and information there can be incredibly useful. I'm a member of many groups on Facebook ranging from those specific to colored pencil, pencil art, wildlife art, wildlife conservation, and artist entrepreneurs.

If you're struggling or feeling alone, check out social media groups for other artists and information.

Have a question you can't seem to figure out with your own research? Ask it! Lots of times other artists will jump in and help you out. They've been there and they're willing to help so that you don't have to waste time and possibly ruin a drawing by testing or trying to figure things out on your own.

It's okay to ask for help.

If you're new to something, don't be shy about it. We were all brand new to everything at one point or another. Speak up and say, "Hey everyone, I'm brand new to *this* technique, or *this* medium. I'm curious what you've found to be the best *this* for this situation? Thanks so much for your help!"

If you want critiques and are ready to have some criticism, post one of your pieces of artwork in an appropriate group and ask for that.

If you're working with colored pencil and want to know what the heck burnishing is, or why it's important to have underlayers, or what on earth wax bloom is, then go to a colored pencil group and ask that. Especially if people in a specific group you like keep talking about something in particular and you don't know what it means, feel free to ask. We've all received help to get where we are and most of us are willing to come to the aid of others in a similar situation.

With networking, comes opportunities!

You never know who you're going to meet, either online or in person. It's important to try and reach out to people in both ways. Go to opening receptions at galleries or for specific artists whose work you enjoy. Attend workshops or conferences or summits. Join a local critique group or create one. Attend networking events, or create your own. At any of these above options you could meet just the person who could hook you up for your next big opportunity!

Just get out of your studio and socialize with like-minded individuals, and you'll be amazed at what comes of it.

Don't forget that your community also involves your audience.

Your clients and customers and fans who love your work might also love getting to meet you. Don't forget that they're part of your community! What better way to make you feel like you're doing something worthwhile than to have a meet and greet with people who love what you do? Doing a local demo or talk or signing is a great way to meet some new fans of your work and to nurture the local ones you already have. Plus, it can boost your self-esteem and pump you up for your next project. Adoring fans are always an instant reason to smile and keep doing what you're doing. Ask them for their opinions about something online (like I did for the cover design of this book), and meet with them in person at receptions, craft fairs, open studios, demos, and more.

16
Comfort Is Overrated

I'll be the first person to admit how frightened I am. Not only do I have a chronic illness that holds me back from doing many of the things I want to do for my business (and in life), I have an anxiety disorder where I push out excess cortisol, the fight or flight hormone. When I get nervous, which is pretty much whenever I go out in public, I quiver and sometimes my skin breaks out into hives.

Sexy, I know.

I'm nervous because even though I grew up with mild anxiety, after I became ill I was mostly bedridden for 6.5 years, starting when I was 18. That's the time I would normally have just begun to break out of my shell at college. Instead I was stuck in a darkened room and forced to not socialize with anyone other than my family and a very few occasions when I saw a friend, for that entire time.

Now that I'm (slowly) starting to feel better, thanks to my current treatment, when I go out in public it's like learning to socialize all over again.

Not only that, I also have the constant threat of my illness flaring up while I'm out there and I'll have to leave suddenly, or I'll be so bad I won't be able to drive and then I'm stranded with a debilitating migraine and/or fatigue. I don't want to be rude, but sometimes I have to leave an event to try and save myself from a horrible situation.

Plus, let's face it, I'm a bit of an introvert most of the time. I have my moments of being extroverted, but most of the time my down time is what gives me energy and socializing is exhausting.

So, let's take all of that and more and wrap it up. It would seem like I should never leave my house, correct? I mean, how could someone who's chronically ill, with anxiety, a chronic headache, who's having to relearn how to socialize going to go out and make a good impression?

It's a valid question, and you might say I have almost every excuse in the book to become a hermit, and it's tempting, but I know better.

The best ways to grow your business are going to involve shuffling up to the edge of your comfort zone and then leaping as far outside of it as you can get.

Despite all the things going against me, I'm a public speaker. I also organize artist networking events and work with sponsors throughout my region to make those happen. I hand deliver proposals to galleries and retailers in my region instead of mailing them because I know it has more of an impact, and I volunteer to help out at galleries. For a while I was the president of the board for an arts non-profit. I personally check in at retailers and galleries that are showing my work, I set up meet & greets with my fans, and I make appearances at events for organizations that I support. I cold call other organizations I want to partner with because I love their mission despite the rejection rate being high, and I attend conferences I know will be useful.

I do all these things despite my anxiety and fear constantly telling me to stop it, stop it right now. I do it because even though I'm WAY outside my comfort zone for each and every thing I just mentioned, it's a huge benefit for my business and for me.

Push yourself to do things that make you nervous or that scare you if you know they're going to help your business.

Public speaking, for example, is a huge ordeal for artists

and non-artists alike. It's scary getting up in front of people. There's no doubt that my hives usually show up when I'm speaking in front of a crowd, but there's ways you can lessen the negative effects of your nerves and up the positive effects. I'll write more about this in an upcoming ebook called *How To Communicate Effectively - For Artists & Creatives* (of which there's a sample chapter in the bonus materials of this book), but I'll explain a little bit of it here, too.

There are key ways to help you overcome your anxiety or nerves and be successful when you're doing anything. Here's a few tips and techniques to help:

- **Body Language.** We all know that if you're confident, your body language will show it, but did you know that if you're not confident, forcing yourself to have confident body language will actually boost your confidence anyway? This is a fantastic technique and one of my favorites. If you're nervous about an interview or speech, for the few minutes before you go on you should strike a "power pose," of which the most common one is the Superman pose with your hands on your hips and your back straight. This type of pose will lower your cortisol levels and boost your testosterone, making you calmer and more confident. And it works.
- **Pay Attention To Your Diaphragm.** Another sign of confidence is when someone breathes deeply and slowly. If you're nervous your breathing tends to get shallow and quick. Fight back by forcing your diaphragm to go lower and take deeper, more normal breaths. This will help calm you and with more oxygen, your muscles and brain will all function better.
- **Yoga & Meditation.** You've probably heard plenty about how good yoga and meditation can be for you, and there's a reason, it's true! For this purpose in particular, yoga poses that are inversions, where your head is down, are the best. Downward dog and forward bends are great for getting blood to your brain and helping calm you

down. Meditation is similar. A daily meditation routine can help you maintain your calm better, but in a pinch, a couple minutes or even 30 seconds of focusing on your breath and nothing else can help calm your nerves.

- **Train Yourself To Think Of Nerves As Excitement.** Everyone gets nervous, but some people interpret the signs of nerves differently than others. If you talk to an athlete, for example, a lot of the time when you ask if they're nervous about their upcoming match they'll tell you no, they're excited! The response to nerves and excitement is extremely similar, if not the same, so start rethinking those nervous symptoms and know they're helping your body function at optimal levels with extra energy because you're excited.

There's plenty more, but those are some of my favorites.

The point is, I know it's scary. I've been there. I'm there all the time, but I don't let it stop me from pursuing my dreams and doing what I need to so I can grow my business. I'm not saying you always need to be outside your comfort zone, fretting and miserable, but if you want to grow and succeed, you better be getting out there regularly.

You'll never know the vast number of opportunities you're missing and the people whose lives you might touch if you don't get out there.

17
Stop Comparing To Others

Something a lot of artists do is compare themselves to other artists, especially when they're starting out. This is a horrible mistake.

There are lots of interviews with professional, highly successful artists who say that they wish someone had told them early on not to compare their own work with that of other artists.

This is me telling you!

This doesn't mean you shouldn't actively view the artwork of others, whether it's the old masters, your peers, or successful contemporary artists. You should. Going to see an art show or even looking at artwork online can be inspiring, especially if you're in a creative drought.

But don't look at another artist's work and feel bad about yourself because yours isn't as good.

Everyone's work is different and unique and we're all at completely different stages in our career.

Sometimes an artist has more experience than you do because they've been doing this for 30+ years. Other times it's an up-and-comer who pops up out of nowhere and hasn't been drawing for very long but is apparently a prodigy because they're whipping out masterpiece after masterpiece.

It doesn't matter.

You do your thing and continue to grow as an artist. The only person you should compare yourself to is you. Are you pushing your limits as an artist? Are you trying new things and going outside your comfort zone? Is your work maturing and you're improving in this technique or that?

Every artist is on their own individual journey. Focus on yours.

This isn't just true for artistic skill.

Don't compare ANYTHING. Not artistic talent, not sales, not number of likes on Facebook, nothing.

Just focus on building your business to the best it can be and maintaining your artistic integrity along the way. You'll find your audience and your adoring fans, it just may take time. And a lot of effort.

Speaking of that up-and-comer who popped up out of nowhere and doesn't seem to have to work nearly as hard for success… don't hate on others' success either.

As artists, we're all in this together. Don't hate on someone else's success, join in the celebration!

If someone you know is having a wildly successful time right now, congratulate them! Then recognize that if they can do it, you can too. What you're seeing with them should be highly motivating because it shows you that this CAN work and you really CAN make a successful business from your artwork.

Then, without being creepy, analyze what that person may be doing differently or better than you are. What triggered their success? Are they advertising? Was it because they are working toward a cause? Is it because they partnered with another organization? Is it partially their blog, their awesome website, their recent interview on TV, their list of awards and publications? What are they doing that seems like it's really adding to their success and how can you follow in their footsteps (without stepping on their toes or outright copying them)?

The best thing you can do for your business is to focus on

being productive, efficient, and smart about prioritizing. Do your research when it comes to what's making other artists successful in their business, and try to build your business in a way that could do the same for you.

Sometimes what works for one artist will be a flop for another.

Experiment. Fail. Experiment some more, until you find what works for you.

Focus on where you are now, and where you want to go, NOT how far you still need to go to get there. If you focus on that long road ahead of you, you'll get overwhelmed, disappointed, and frustrated. Instead, continue working on your plan and moving forward one Step Goal at a time.

18
Marketing

Business is a numbers game. The more people who see your work, the more potential buyers for your work. It's that simple.

And yet it's not simple.

How do you get your artwork or craft out in front of the right people? Not just the right people, but the right people, at the right time, in the right place?

We all know that if no one sees your amazing artwork, then no one can buy it. If everything is constantly sitting in piles in your studio collecting dust, then how can you expect customers to come along and purchase it?

There are a lot of extremely talented artists who never turn their work into a successful business because they don't understand or focus on marketing.

If you want to be successful, it's suggested that you spend HALF your time on marketing.

I know, that sounds like a lot. But it makes sense if you think about it. Marketing isn't something you do once that works and suddenly your business is booming. Marketing requires constant effort and time and a consistent message being sent out into the world for people to find and hopefully fall in love with your work.

This chapter is just an overview, whereas the next few

chapters go into detail about some specific aspects of marketing.

There's more to marketing than social media.

Social media is great and there's a whole chapter coming up on just that, but don't downplay other types of marketing. There's traditional marketing, there's other ways to market online, and there's building partnerships, etc. Social media can be very powerful when used right. If you feel that you have a knack for a certain social media platform, like Instagram, go for it and utilize it as much as you can, especially if you're seeing good results from those efforts. But if you're spending an hour a day on social media posts and you're not seeing any sales from it, it may be time to switch it up, or at least talk to someone who is doing well with that to see how they're succeeding.

There's a ton of resources for artists when it comes to building your business and marketing your artwork. Here's a few of my favorites that you might want to check out:

~ **Art Marketing News – Barney Davey.** Barney Davey is someone who consistently puts out useful information about marketing your artwork. He does podcasts with **Xanadu Gallery** owner Jason Horejs talking about different aspects of the art market, he's written books on the subject, including **Guerilla Marketing**, and he has great information on his blog.

From his website www.artmarketingnews.com: "*Barney Davey* provides advice to artists to grow their career through his books, blog posts, workshops, online training, consulting and more."

~ **Artsy Shark – Carolyn Edlund.** Carolyn Edlund runs this art blog with featured artists three times a week and business articles every Tuesday and Thursday. The artist features is something you might want to look into and the business articles always have some great and useful info. She's also the director for the **Arts Business Institute**, which has a great blog and provides fantastic workshops.

From her website www.artsyshark.com: "I'm Carolyn Edlund, the founder of Artsy Shark. My mission is to inspire artists to build better businesses."

~ **The Art Biz Coach – Alyson Stanfield.** Alyson Stanfield is a professional who's down to earth, honest, and welcoming. Her blog, the Art Biz Coach, is full of useful information and she offers coaching to artists who want to grow their business.

From her website www.artbizcoach.com: "I work with hundreds of visual artists every year in my online classes, membership programs, 1-on-1 consultations, and live events."

~**The Abundant Artist – Cory Huff.** Cory Huff is the mastermind behind this website and they offer online courses, coaching, and a lot of great, free information for artists trying to build their business and sell their work online.

From his website www.theabundantartist.com: "The Abundant Artist's mission is not only about teaching talented artists to sell their art online, but about dispelling the starving artist myth."

~ **Fine Art Tips - Lori McNee.** Lori McNee is a visual artist who has also gained a large social media and online following and created the Fine Art Tips website and blog to help out other artists.

From her website www.finearttips.com: "Fine art tips, the premier online resource for the working artist. Fine art tips, marketing and social media advice for the professional & aspiring artist."

Plus there's a LOT more, so do some Googling to find them. Also, I'm a huge fan of Entrepreneur Magazine, Forbes, and Inc. Magazine online articles for news and ideas about marketing in general that are not art-specific. There's also a lot of great TED talks on any subject, from anxiety to business.

A lot of artists don't like marketing or really anything to do with the business side of their artwork. Like we learned about working styles earlier, sometimes there are things you're just not good at no matter how much you try to force yourself to do them.

Maybe you're this type of artist and maybe that means you should hire a representative or an agent to handle your marketing for you. Just remember if you do this, take the time to find someone reputable and professional. You want your artwork and your business in the best of hands, so get references, see their success rates, find out exactly what they do and how they get paid and if it's a fair arrangement. You probably want to get an art-friendly lawyer involved to look over everything before you sign.

There's a lot of scammers out there, so be careful.

Maybe you're like me and your brain is more interested in this type of work. If so, great! This means, if you have the time, you can market yourself.

The biggest difficulty is finding a balance between creating your artwork and marketing your business.

You don't want to spend so much time creating new work that you forget to market yourself because your business will stall and you won't be making any sales. The same goes for the other way around. You don't want to be so focused on marketing that you forget to make new work and your customers get bored. They want to see what you're working on and new material! Make them happy by showing it to them through your marketing.

Want more on marketing and communication? Check out my book: How To Communicate Effectively - For Artists & Creatives where I go into detail about marketing materials, writing proposals, artist statements, branding, grant writing, and much more.

19
Social Media

A lot of artists are falling into the trap that social media marketing is all they need to do. That's not the case. Other forms of marketing can be as effective, if not more effective than social media, but in today's age, social media can be a very effective tool.

Marketing is all about growing your audience, and social media can be a great tool for that.

With social media, it's all about the number of likes, follows, shares, and pins. But it's also about content. No one is going to like your post if it doesn't have interesting content that they, well, like.

With Facebook as an example, we all know that a like is good, a comment is great, and a share is spectacular. But what makes a person go from just clicking the like button and continuing to scroll, to liking it, commenting on it, clicking the link, and sharing it on their own page?

Content.

This can mean a number of things, as each person has their own idea of what's "shareable" content. The idea is to figure out what your target market and customers think is shareable (and hopefully buyable) content and then put out a consistent flow of things they like.

Certain things that are extremely popular right now are

things like: time-lapse videos of a drawing/painting/sculpture, live videos of an artist at work, images from the studio, blog posts about your process, posts that involve animals in any funny or cute way, and new work either just finished or being created.

These post types are popular across the board, so you might want to get in on some of that if you haven't already, as your audience will probably love it. But there may also be things specific to your page. For example, my mission involves supporting wildlife conservation efforts with some of my sales, so sometimes I'll post a really cool video or article relating to that topic to share with my fans and remind them of my passion for animals.

The more your content gets shared, the more people who will see it, and it's all back to that numbers game of marketing. The more people who see your work, the more sales you're likely to make.

Speaking of sales, make sure your social media audience has an easy way to buy from you!

Make sure your website or Etsy shop or wherever you sell work online is highly visible on your social media pages. Make it as easy as possible for someone to buy your work if they find you via social media. The more steps someone has to take to get to a sales page, the less likely they'll follow through. People have a ridiculously low attention span, so quicker and easier is better.

Now you can even add a shop to places like Facebook where they can buy products or artwork directly from your Facebook page, as long as it's a business page. You do have a business page, right? Not just your own personal page? That's important as it helps you gain a bigger audience, you can use the insights to see the traffic on your page, and it lends to your ever-important online credibility.

Or you can make it easy for a customer to buy something by providing links in each of your posts, allowing them to contact you to pay via a private message, or posting directly from your website/shop.

Sometimes people get overwhelmed with social media. Between Facebook, Twitter, LinkedIn, Instagram, Pinterest, Snapchat, Tumblr, and more, you may be asking yourself, how will I ever have the time to do this?

My answer is don't.

At least, not all of it.

I suggest you start out by choosing two platforms that you like best. My two favorites for artists and creatives are Facebook and Instagram because they're so visual. As a writer, my other favorite is Twitter. Pinterest is also pretty visual, so if you have a lot of products that could be 'pinned' to different types of boards, say if you're a wedding gown designer, or jewelry maker, or pottery master, that might be a good one for you. LinkedIn can also be good for making professional connections, like with gallery owners, retailers, curators, etc.

Whatever you choose, start out with two and focus on doing those two well, instead of trying to do all of them and doing them poorly. Once you choose your two, start uploading regular, interesting content. It doesn't always need to be new work, it can be products you're making, a new product for sale, works in progress, videos, photos of you working, blog posts, ideas you have related to your art, questions you have for your fans, etc.

Try not to let social media be a time-suck.

There's a lot of content out there, and between cool artwork and funny animal videos that other people are posting, it can be easy to get sucked into your computer screen for an hour or two or three and then you no longer have time for the rest of your work.

Plan what you're going to post, post it, scroll around quickly to stay updated on what's happening, and then close it down and move on to your next task. No excuses! Don't spend too much time on this and don't check it too often during the day. It's like we talked about with email, have 3 times a day when you check it and respond to people and then put it aside and work productively at your other important tasks.

Don't forget what we talked about in the chapter about networking too, social media can be a great way to help build a community. Not only can it build your audience of adoring fans and raving customers, it can be a place to talk with other artists and gain wisdom and inspiration.

It can also be a place where haters come out of the woodwork and start throwing rocks at you. Like we said in a previous chapter, don't get caught up in that either. Don't engage, either remove the comments or just ignore them and move on.

Social media has a lot of good things going for it, and a lot of negatives. Learn where you might get tripped up (for me it's letting it distract me from other work I need to do), and recognize what you need to do to minimize the negatives for yourself. If you're having trouble remembering to post regularly, set reminders for yourself until it becomes a habit (just don't post 18 times a day, once is fine). If you're not sure what content to post, check out what other artists are doing and see if you can do something similar.

If you don't use social media, you're going to be missing out on a huge market of people. If you get your content shared, it's equivalent to that person endorsing your product because they're essentially telling all their friends that they like you and your work and by sharing it they're suggesting it to them, just like they might while talking over dinner. Except this is even better because if someone is interested, all they have to do is click on the shared link and be directed to you and your work.

20
Email Marketing

If you've done much research on marketing lately you'll read a lot about email marketing in particular. What is email marketing? It's exactly what it sounds like, where you send someone a series of emails to market to them directly.

Sounds easy enough, right?

Well, the difficult part here is getting those email addresses, known as your email list.

This is far easier said than done.

There are a number of ways you can build your email list, but here are some of my favorites:

- **Put A Signup On Your Website.** People can only be on your email list if they know where to sign up, so make sure you have a clear signup form on your website. This can be on the side of your website, at the top, or even a popup that comes out after they've been on your site for a certain amount of time, maybe 15 seconds.

- **Use Incentives.** In order to incentivize people to sign up for your list, give them something in return. Offer a short ebook, or some other digital product that they can easily download just for signing up to your list. This works incredibly well, but make sure whatever you're giving away is still good-quality content. If they sign up for your list and get something that is mediocre, they're not likely to stay on the list or want whatever else you have to offer.

- **Partner With Someone.** A great way to build your audience for your emails is to partner with someone else. This will typically be someone who's not a direct competitor but who has an audience that will like your work. (There's a whole chapter on this later.)
- **Promotions.** Offer your customers a coupon, a discount, or something else if they sign up for your newsletter list, and promote it across platforms. Maybe try a Facebook or Instagram ad to reach a new audience and get some new emails.

Building a list can be slow and agonizing. Sometimes you'll do something, like hold a webinar, and you'll get a rush of new people signing up, but then it'll die down again. This is the same with any marketing you do. That's why in order to keep building your list you need to keep doing those things that are working.

Then, of course, you need to figure out what you're going to be writing to those email subscribers.

Sometimes it's best to have multiple email lists. If you're an artist but you're also a business coach, it might be good to have two separate lists, one for your audience interested in your business advice, and another for the audience interested in your artwork.

You need to email consistently, but not so much that it's annoying. Figuring out what that means can be tricky because some people may want to hear from you more than others. Sometimes the way people handle this problem is by asking how often you want to hear from them. For some of the lists I've signed up for, they've given me the option of daily, weekly, and monthly to get notifications and information. I usually choose weekly.

Sometimes a monthly newsletter is all you need. It depends on your business. Some businesses thrive on two emails a week, some daily. If you're a weekly blogger, maybe you should consider notifying your list when your weekly blog has been posted and add in other pertinent information with those weekly emails for whatever else you have going on.

The best thing about email marketing is that it gives people a chance to get to know you. It allows people to hear what you have to say from a distance and decide if they like you, then gradually get to know you better and what you're about, and then by the time you're trying to sell them something they already know they like and trust you and your chances of a sale are better.

It's a warm call vs. a cold call. It's cold when you ask for their email address, but within a short amount of time, they'll read your content and get to know you enough where when you pitch them something they might like to buy, it's warm.

Keep in mind that a big list is great and that's the goal, but you want to emphasize quality over quantity.

Don't go buying a list of names. That's never a good idea. Instead, take the time to build and nurture your own list from the ground up. It's better to have 250 people who are really interested in what you have to say and are active followers than to have 10,000 people who don't care or pay attention.

That being said, you're also going to get unsubscribers. That's okay! Remember the definition of rejection? What you are offering wasn't quite what that person was looking for, which is fine because if that's true, you don't want them on your list anyway. You only want people who are actively paying attention to what you have to say. There's no need to waste your time on anyone else.

One main thing to think about when you're crafting your emails is to imagine you're writing to one person, not the whole list. Emails are meant to be personal, so try to make yours as personal sounding as possible without having to craft different emails for different people. Most programs, like Mailchimp or Constant Contact, allow you to insert the subscriber's name in the email as if you're writing to them directly.

For example:

"Hi [first-name],

Corrina here to let you know that email marketing is a great way to build your online business...."

A lot of programs will provide you with a shortcut that looks like the above when you write it, the [first-name], and it tells the program to insert the name of each individual subscriber in that part of the email.

You've probably seen this in plenty of emails for which you've subscribed, and it works. It personalizes the email, even when you know it's because of a program code, it still has a positive effect.

Of course, I've seen this go drastically wrong too. Sometimes if someone tries to do this shortcut code and does it wrong, it can make your email look unprofessional because instead of saying the person's name, it says some sort of garble, or it literally says "Hey there first-name."

Therefore, TEST your emails before you send them out to your whole list. Send them to yourself to make sure they're formatted correctly and look at them in the preview mode provided by the program you're using.

Not to put too much pressure on you, but if you go and ask professional marketers what the number one best online marketing tool is right now, they will almost all tell you email marketing. This doesn't mean you have to master it overnight, it takes a long time to build an audience. But keep building it because it can pay off as time goes on.

Your email list could prove to be one of the most important sales tools to build and grow your business.

21
The Importance Of Branding

When you say "Branding" a lot of people make a scrunchy face with a look that says, what does that even really mean?

Branding means keeping your marketing message clear and consistent.

This can take a lot of forms. For example, my artwork really pops against a black background, despite most people saying black backgrounds are a bad idea. Because mine works so well that way, better than most, I use a black background for my website. Now, in order to create a consistent, branded look, my business cards have a black background, with the same fonts as my website, a lot of my marketing materials have black backgrounds (postcards, rack cards, invitations, calendars, etc.), and when I do a craft show I use black table cloths and black panels to show my work on. This is a simple visual trick to make them all unified and let people know it's all part of the same company.

Branding let's people know that everything you're doing is connected to each other and part of the same company.

If you always paint portraits and suddenly you throw in a landscape, it may throw off your audience because it's atypical for your brand. Likewise if you have white business cards with no images next to brochures that are black and full of images next to posters that look different from those, you're not being consistent with your brand. Keep the look of your marketing materials consistent. They don't have to be exactly the same, but it should be clear when they're lined up that they are from the same company.

Another part of branding is your logo. Don't have a logo? You might want to make one. If you sell products like greeting cards and calendars and mugs and mousepads, an easy way to help with branding is to add your logo on the back or in the corner of each product.

This goes for everything you do. If your social media pages are totally different from each other and your website, that's not very good branding. Instead, have the same color theme, the same profile image, and your logo and your name or the name of your company on everything.

Branding helps you build credibility. When you are showing a consistent face to the public with your website and other online pages, as well as your printed marketing materials, it makes you seem trustworthy. People feel like you are a professional who has high-quality products and will likely have good customer service.

Marketing is about telling a story.

People love stories. A great way to brand yourself and market your business is to share you own personal story. Mixed with the branding above, this will make you not only seem credible and professional, but interesting and personable as well.

I'm lucky (in a horrible sort of way) that my story comes easily. I was definitely not an artist growing up, but then I fell chronically, debilitatingly ill when I was 18. When I turned 20 I was still undiagnosed and in excruciating daily pain, unable to do much of anything. One day, I picked up a pencil and a leftover piece of poster board and started to sketch. I don't know why, other than I was looking for something, anything I could physically do. From then on, a little at a time as my body would allow, I taught myself to draw from the confines of my bed, creating realistic, vibrant wildlife portraits with colored pencils.

That's the extremely shortened version of my story. If you

want to hear more about it, I'm also writing a memoir, but until that comes out check out my blog on my website: **www.corrinathurston. com**

You can see how I started drawing is a naturally interesting story that draws a lot of people in. People are interested in my artwork first, then they're intrigued by my medium because my artwork looks more like a painting or photo than colored pencil, which is shocking for some viewers, and then they're fascinated by my story and drawn in even further.

My story makes me memorable. When I'm at an exhibit or an art fair where I might meet people, what I hear a lot is: "Aren't you that colored pencil artist? The artwork that's so detailed?" or "Aren't you the sick artist who started drawing from bed?" or "You're that animal artist! The sick one who creates those crazy colored pencil drawings."

Yes, yes I am.

At first it was a little unnerving to have people walk up to me and ask me if I was that sick artist they heard about. Not the most flattering sounding question, but accurate nonetheless. Now I've learned to embrace it as part of my story, part of what makes me memorable beyond just my artwork. Now people think of me when they think of animals, artists, colored pencils, entrepreneurship, speaking, chronic illness, lyme disease, etc.

So the question is, what's your story?

It's okay if you don't have a story that automatically comes to you and explains exactly how you began drawing and is memorable and interesting. Think about it for a few days. Write down some ideas and piece them together.

If your story is that you just love to create jewelry because it's pretty, then you have a lot of work to do because that doesn't tell your audience anything.

Your audience wants you to let them in. My best and most popular blog posts are the ones that are the most personal to me. I wrote a blog post in around Thanksgiving in 2016, not long after starting my blog, titled:*An Emotional Post This Thanksgiving - My*

That post got more interest than my entire website had in the few weeks leading up to it. People went gaga over it because I was honest and delved deep into my own life to talk about how I've become happier than I ever have been, despite my chronic illness. It touched people and apparently made some of them cry.

That's memorable.

If you can create content that has people on the edge of their seat or with tears in their eyes or laughing or saying wow, then you're hitting the jackpot for being memorable. And if you're memorable, people will keep coming back and they'll keep sharing your content with other people and your audience will grow.

To figure out your own story, think about how you became an artist. Have you been drawing since you were little? Did you always have a knack for creativity? Maybe you have a drawing you did when you were 7 and it shows an extreme amount of skill for that age. If so, share it!

Maybe drawing or painting or sculpting was always a hobby for you but never an option for a career. What changed? Did you get sick of your day job? Did you take a workshop that changed your mind or have an epiphany moment?

Maybe there's a quote you really love that sums up how you feel about being an artist. Maybe you've always known this was your path and you went to school for it and have been creating for years with lots of awards and a degree and portfolio.

All of this is great to start with, but then you have to get into the nitty gritty of how your story is different. What makes you or your artwork different and special? Maybe it's that you are mission-driven and you really care about a certain cause so you create artwork with that cause in mind and some of your proceeds go to support it. Maybe you started drawing in order to give yourself a therapeutic outlet and now you teach art therapy to others in your community and share what you learned and how beneficial and amazing it can be and seeing the smiles on the faces of people who are otherwise in dark places is what drives you, etc.

Keep thinking. Keep pecking away at why you're an artist when there are so many other things you could have done. Then share that with the world.

Let your audience in and be personable and open and honest and kind. Don't be afraid of what others will think, just be you and you will touch someone's life with your honesty.

The biggest reasons for branding are:
- So people can recognize your work immediately
- So people know you're a professional
- So people feel comfortable with you
- So you gain credibility
- So you are memorable
- So people can trust you

People buy things from those they know and trust. If you are consistent with your branding and you let people in to see what's behind the scenes in your studio and your life, they'll feel like they know and trust you. Then they're more likely to buy from you and you're off and running to grow your business.

The better you are at this, the more it will show in your word of mouth sales, your shares on social media, and in the number of people who reach out to you. I have to say, it's a great feeling when someone (or many someones) reach out to you to let you know that you've inspired them or that they love your work or that they find you fascinating. It's even better when it comes from a paying customer, but it's still pretty great coming from anyone.

Trust me, I'm not someone who thought I would inspire other people, especially as an artist or entrepreneur. Growing up, those two things were nowhere in sight, and I was fine with that. I was going to pursue Biology and Anthropology and have a double-major and be a rock star female scientist. There's nothing wrong with that, and I encourage anyone who wants to do so, but my illness changed all that.

The only way I got where I am today is by adapting to my circumstances.

I know my path to get here is part of what made me who I am and therefore I'm open about it. If I can help people in any way, that's awesome. If some people just find me interesting, that's fine too.

In this world full of bad news and worse reality, it's nice to be told stories that, even though in general they're not good (falling chronically ill and being sick for a decade, etc.), there's a silver lining and good things have come from it and someone is making the best of their situation. We need good news. Share with your audience your good news, along with the bad. Be real. Don't make things up, you have a reputation to keep. Just let them peek behind the curtain sometimes.

<h1 style="text-align:center">22
How and Why To Build
Partnerships</h1>

Like we talked about earlier, connections can be the key to you finding a great opportunity you otherwise might not have known about. Those connections can also be turned into partnerships if you play your cards right.

There's a lot of different types of partnerships, and the main goal is to grow your audience by tapping into the audience of someone else.

The best partnerships are with people or organizations who are not direct competitors with you, but whose audience has similar interests.

For example, if you're a wildlife artist you don't want to try and partner necessarily with another wildlife artist, unless of course it's for a cooperative project. Instead, think about other companies that have a similar audience. What about zoos? Nature museums? Or if you donate to wildlife conservation, find other companies, like those for apparel, or jewelry, or other products, that also donate to a similar or the same cause and reach out to them.

A lot of this type of reaching out will likely be cold-calling, which means your success rate is going to drop. For the best results, start following a company or person you're interested in on social media. Become an active member of their following so your name starts showing up. Comment on posts you find particularly interesting, and comment as your own art page, so they recognize that you're a business too.

After a while of being engaged on their pages, drop them a note saying how much you enjoy their company, or how much you appreciate that they support the same causes you do, etc. Just be friendly and truthful and courteous.

If they get back to you, great! Then you can say something like, "I've been a fan of your company for a while now and really enjoy what you do as it's a goal for my own business to do *this* as well. Do you think you'd have any interest in partnering for a joint promotion on Facebook? It would involve *this and this...*"

Take your time to get to know this other company and if possible, the actual person you're writing to. Think seriously if they might be interested in what you're offering. If you don't have a ton of followers and they do, it's obvious what you're getting out of the deal, so make it clear what they could get out of it too.

No business will partner with you if they're not getting something out of it too.

Don't fret, you don't need a million followers to be a good partner. You're partnering to increase your audience, remember? But maybe you have a product that their audience will really like and you're willing to give some away to them for free?

Every business is looking for great content for their audience. If you have great content or products to share, make that known in your pitch.

Speaking of content, guest blogging is a fantastic way to reach new audiences as well.

Do you know a blog that accepts guest posts where their audience might like what you have to offer? Pitch them with a guest post idea! Write them a proposal about a post idea you have that would be beneficial for their audience, and explain exactly *what* that idea is and *how* it benefits them.

Bloggers are always looking for great new content, so if you can provide it, they'll be happy to post it and credit you with a link to your website or blog or book or whatever you provide to them. Trust me, you just saved them a bunch of work! Not only will they be thankful, you've also just made a great connection with someone who has a good audience. Follow them on Facebook and other social media sites to keep that relationship alive and it may be helpful for you in the future in some way as well.

Another way to reach a bigger audience through a partnership is to reach out to influencers.

"Influencers" is a vague term, but essentially it's anyone who has influence with their opinion, meaning celebrities, experts, and other professionals who have an audience of people who follow their advice.

The most recognizable form of this is product placement. Have you ever seen a celebrity, on Instagram especially, post a photo of themselves wearing a t-shirt that's for a charity/cause, or shoes from a company they love, or which body-shaper company they like, or juice company, etc? It's very common to see a celebrity promoting something just by posting a photo of themselves with the product and saying how much they love it. Because they have an audience of people who eat up everything they say and do and follow their advice, this is the best and most effective type of word-of-mouth advertising out there.

For example, in commercials. When you see the commercial of Lebron James drinking and promoting Sprite, it's because Sprite knows that Lebron has a huge following and he is an influencer. Having his name and face with that of Sprite automatically lifts Sprite's ratings in the minds of Lebron fans. This is influencer marketing.

Now you're thinking, well that's fine and dandy, but I don't have millions of dollars to spend on a commercial with Lebron James. True, but that's not the only way you can reach out to influencers, and not all influencers need to be as big as Lebron James.

Maybe you know a gallery owner who has a newsletter that goes out to 1000 people in the region and you want to reach out to them to see if they have any interest in partnering with you. Or maybe you reach out to a minor celebrity and offer to send them free products for them to test out and post about on Instagram.

You can always start small and work your way up. Know someone who is active on Facebook and even though they don't have a ton of followers, their followers are highly engaged? Ask them if they'd like a free print or product and if they'd be willing to post about it on Facebook and tag you. Then find someone else like that, and someone else, and keep moving up to influencers who have more and more followers.

Every industry has influencers. Who are the experts in your field or a field that is connected to yours? Who are the top people in your local community, regional community, and national community who might be able and willing to help promote your brand?

Influencers not only have avid followers, they have great connections. Influencers tend to know people, and when you know people you can get your foot in the door much more easily. And keep in mind, the more people you know and the more followers you get, the more of an influencer you become too.

Another relationship you should seek out and foster is that with the media.

Media exposure is great for businesses, and most of the time, it's free. If you have an exhibit coming up or an event, reach out to your local newspapers to see if they want to write a story about it.

This is where your story, what makes you unique and interesting and different, comes in handy. Without a hook or background story, the media may not want to cover your event. What's in it for them? What's in it for their readers or viewers?

Partnering is all about mutual satisfaction. You are able to tap into a new, bigger audience, and your partner gets something in return.

When it comes to the media, your partner is looking for a compelling story idea.

The media, similar to bloggers, need compelling content to keep their audience happy. If you can provide that, great! They'll be more than happy to partner with you for a story. If you just have an opening reception of your abstract work in a coffee shop and no story to go with it, probably not so much.

My first media story was an accident. It was 2011 and I had been drawing for a year and sick for three years, still without a diagnosis. I'd posted a little of my artwork on Facebook and was getting a good response, so I had my mom (keep in mind I'm still mostly bedridden here) stop in at a local coffee shop that I knew showed artwork and asked if they'd be interested in a display of my work. They said yes.

I had started drawing a year before and I could only do a little at a time, so I had 14 drawings I had finished. I used 12 to make my display in the coffee shop, starting with the third drawing I'd done.

Let's take a moment to recognize that that's pretty much unheard of. I was a huge exception to the rule. If you're looking at your earliest drawings and thinking how could someone possibly display their earliest work when they were just learning how to draw or paint, you're not alone. It shocks everyone, and it added to my story. But like I said, it's the exception to the rule, so if you're comparing yourself to my quick progress, don't. Don't compare anything like that, remember? But if you DO have a quick progress like that, perhaps you can use it as part of your story?

So the next thing I did was make my work presentable by matting and framing it, and then created little labels for each one. **Then I wrote a short press release for my local newspaper.**

The press release wasn't anything special, it just said that I was having my artwork displayed at the local coffee shop in Barre, VT, known as Espresso Bueno, and that I'd been sick for 3 years and had started drawing as a constructive outlet with colored pencil. I included a photo of one of my best drawings, my Sea Turtle, and that was that.

I wasn't sure if they would print anything at all. I was

displaying in a coffee shop, not a gallery, I was a completely unknown artist and honestly didn't think of myself as an "artist" for another few years, and I was just doing this to keep myself sane.

The next day one of the newspaper editors contacted me to ask a couple questions and then asked if they could turn my press release into an interview and article. Of course, I said yes. (Never turn down free publicity!)

The day the display went up, I brought three people with me to hang my artwork because I didn't have that kind of energy, and the writer/photographer from the Times Argus newspaper came along. I sat in the corner directing my helpers for the hanging process and answered his questions about my illness, my current diagnosis, how I started drawing, why colored pencil, etc.

This turned into a 2-page story in the newspaper the next week with three photos and another local newspaper picked it up after that, conducting their own interview of me, and other places contacted me to see if I wanted to display my artwork there as well.

All because I took 15 minutes to write a short press release to my local paper.

So take the time. Even if you think it's too small of an event for the newspaper to take notice, write the press release. Look up a template for formatting online and write to them, or just send them an email. If you provide an interesting story, they might just latch on! And the worst that could happen is they don't get back to you or they say no thanks.

The one thing to keep in mind about the media is that you don't have much control over how they present you.

You have to be very careful what you say and how you say it when speaking with the media because if they can get an even juicier story because you accidentally just said something bashing another artist or gallery, then that might be what they run with instead of the awesomeness of your display.

So be careful. **Here's some things to keep in mind:**

- Be polite and courteous. If you're nice to them, they'll usually be nice to you.

- Provide great content.
- Speak in sound bites. Remember, they're looking for quotes. Speak in a way that is conscious of what they need and make it easier for them.
- Think before you speak. Anything can be quoted, so make sure you think before you speak. One misstep could mean an article that is skewed in a negative way.
- The media is free publicity! Relish your relationships with those in the media because if they like you and they're good at their job, they are a fantastic connection and anything a newspaper or television show presents about you is free publicity for you. Why pay for an ad that people will look over when you can get an entire story written about you?
- Start locally and then expand. It's important to start with your local media and then expand out to regional and then national. Not only does it give you more practice as you give interviews locally, it will boost your portfolio and resume and you'll be more likely to be able to land a bigger interview down the road.

You'll notice in this chapter I haven't said much about galleries. But they're an obvious choice for a partnership, correct? Well, maybe.

The art world is changing and most galleries have yet to change with it. There's a huge and surprising number of people who now buy their artwork online instead of with galleries, or they prefer to go to coops and unique gift stores and the personal studios of artists.

It used to be that if you could get represented by a gallery or a handful of galleries around the region, you were all set. That partnership would provide you with income and the credibility of the gallery and your business would be safe.

That's changed. Gallery sales have dropped as online sales and sales made directly by the artist have jumped. You no longer

NEED a gallery to represent you, you can represent yourself.

That being said, partnering with a gallery can still be a great thing for you and your business, assuming you choose one that works for you. Some galleries have done a great job adapting and keeping up with the pace of the market, changing their business model and supporting artists in new ways. Look for that in your partnerships and make sure that you can provide enough artwork to keep the relationship viable. Some galleries need new work every month. Can you do that? Make sure you know exactly what they expect from you and know what to expect from them.

Some people are saying galleries are a dying breed. Only time will tell, but I doubt it. I'm betting that galleries will make a comeback, but they might be a little different than they used to be.

Partnering with a gallery might not be the golden nugget for your business that it used to be, but depending on your artwork and the specific gallery, it could be one of your many streams of income and good for your business. Just don't expect it to throw your career into overdrive and make you instantly successful.

By building partnerships with other people, companies, influencers, and the media you're able to expand your reach drastically. All you need to do is provide those potential partners with either great content for their audience, or something else in return for some form of joint promotion.

You can do this! Don't be afraid to jump outside your comfort zone and reach out. You'll get a lot of rejection, but for the ones whom you do find a connection, they'll thank you for reaching out.

*In the Bonus Materials at the end of this book is a useful guide I've put together specifically for partnerships: **12 Questions To As Before Creating A Partnership.***

23
Useful Persistence

Persistence, determination, courage, hard work… these are things we hear all the time. It's key phrases people put on their job applications and say are their highest qualities, but they've been overused. Everyone seems to feel as though they are persistent, but I rarely see people who are truly persistent, or who are persistent in a useful way.

That's the key, not only do you need to be persistent, you need to be persistent in a useful way for your business.

Sometimes this is mistaken for just not giving up. That's great in certain circumstances, but you need to learn when you should persist and when you should scrap a project and move on.

If you're working on a piece of marketing that you do all the time, for instance you give a lot of stuff away for giveaways or charity auctions because you think the exposure will be good, that's fine. But you need to measure the success of those actions. If you've given away 5 prints or pieces of artwork to charity auctions and you haven't seen a single bump in your website views or correspondence or sales that is directly because of those donations, then why are you doing it?

Now this is tricky because of course there's charities that you want to help out whether or not it helps your business. If you can afford that and it makes you happy, then do it, that's great. But if you have super limited resources and you're giving things away all the time and not seeing anything in return, you need to reevaluate your strategy and it's likely you should stop doing that.

That doesn't sound like persistence, does it? Giving up? There's a little part of your brain that says, but the next one might be the one where that exposure actually pays off! How can I not try and see? Maybe if I just do enough of them my name will get out there and it'll start paying off. I can't give up yet!

Yes you can. There are other ways to get your name out there, and seeing as this way isn't getting you any new sales, most of them are probably better.

This is where persistence that's USEFUL comes into play.

Being persistent in the way I described above is not useful to your business, instead it's hurting your business because you're giving out product you spent time and money on for little or nothing in return. That's a bad investment.

Instead, you need to be persistent with things that will actually grow and help your business. Things like building partnerships, getting your name out there with displays and publications, and building a community. These are things that are proven to help any type of business, so spend time on them.

Keep getting rejected from galleries? If you think that having your work in galleries will help your business then keep sending your materials to more and more galleries. Hire a consultant to analyze your proposals to see what you might be doing wrong. Persist.

Or, build up your artist resume by looking for alternative exhibit locations to persist in a different way. Some of my most lucrative displays were actually at hospitals, coffee shops, and other businesses. Maybe that's something you want to pursue as well? Just remember these are public spaces and damage to your artwork is more likely. This is why I typically display high-quality prints instead of originals, which also allows me to have multiple displays going at once in different places, plus if something gets damaged it's easily replaceable, unlike an original.

I also know artists who would NEVER display in a restaurant because it's not 'fine art' enough or they don't want to create prints and they're worried about damage, etc. That's fine too, to each their own. I liked displaying in common areas like that because it got my name and my artwork out in front of people who might not typically walk into a gallery. I might not sell a $4000 drawing from a coffee shop, but I could sell multiple $250 prints and get requests for commissions. I find that coffee shops and restaurants bring in an eclectic range of people, so you are putting your artwork out in front of a lot of potential customers for one thing or another, as long as you make your display noticeable and it doesn't fall into the background of the room. People don't go to a coffee shop to buy artwork, they're there to get coffee to help get through their busy day. So make sure your artwork jumps out at them as they're waiting in line. Give them something to look at and have them thinking about how great it would be to look at that image every day in their office or home.

Make sure your work has your contact information on it, and better yet, business cards that people can take.

One of the best ways of persisting is by following up. If you sent a proposal to a gallery, make sure to follow up and make sure the curator received it and let them know if they have any questions, to feel free to contact you. This makes you seem like a professional and reminds them to get back to you if they haven't already.

Just make sure to wait a few weeks before reaching out. Curators are busy people and if you sent a proposal on Monday and then contact them on Tuesday, they're going to feel pressured and will likely have not even seen your proposal yet. Give them a couple weeks and then reach out.

Another place where you should follow up and be persistent (without badgering) is "almost" sales. Was there someone at a craft show who looked at one of your paintings for a long time, contemplating whether or not to get it, and despite all your efforts, walked away? Make sure you're able to reach back out to them.

I had a woman come into a booth of mine one summer

and she loved my work but she was disappointed I didn't have an elephant drawing, so she started to walk away. I walked up to her as she was leaving to let her know that an elephant was in fact something I would be doing soon, so if she wanted to sign up for my newsletter, she'd be notified as soon as I had an elephant drawing ready. So she did, nonchalantly, with no real intention to buy a piece, and when I finished my elephant drawing I made sure she was on the list of people who heard about it right away. A sale of a print followed.

Every time someone seems interested but is wavering, get their information and follow up. Offer them a coupon code for joining your email list, or some other incentive. If they're on your email list and they see your name and your artwork every week or month, they may just change their minds and buy that piece after all.

This is persistence that's useful. Following up, sending out more proposals, not letting rejection hold you back.

One reason people have trouble persisting is because of failure. Rejection, failure, and possible humiliation are all things that stop people from persisting and achieving success.

Don't let rejection or failure hold you back. Both of them are necessary in order to succeed.

If you have a great idea for a project and you just KNOW it's going to be successful and you work on it for months, perfecting it and making it great, and then you put it out to market and it flops… that can instantly deflate you. What happened? This piece or product is amazing and yet nobody cares! You spent weeks and months working on it and it's not bringing in any income.

This happens. It means you may not know your audience or your market as well as you think you do. That's okay. You either need to relearn your current audience, or start building a new one and find those people who think that new product is as awesome as you think it is.

Maybe you need two audiences, one for your abstract work and one for your sculpture, or one for your writing and one for your painting. If you have work that varies from your other work, your audience might already be split. Do some polling of your fans to see what they like best. Sometimes when an artist varies greatly from their usual style, their audience that they've cultivated gets confused and isn't sure what to think.

If a product you launch fails, it's not the end of the world. In fact, it's going to happen to everyone along the way, especially in the beginning. That's why most people give up. Part of it might be you just don't understand marketing yet and therefore that product didn't get out in front of the right people, so no one bought it. It could be that the product needs some tweaks of it's own because it's not as convenient or functional as you think it is.

Not every product will do well, or every service. Don't let that get you down. Move on to the next one (only after you know that this one is officially dead). If a product definitely isn't working no matter what you do, even after giving it some time to gain momentum and playing it up in all your marketing materials, then put it to rest and move on to the next one, making sure the next one isn't too similar to this one.

The point of all this is to keep trying. Keep working toward those goals you have and keep moving forward even if you fail. That's persistence. It doesn't mean keep banging your head against the wall, it means keep looking for ways to build your business, one opportunity at a time.

No one thing is likely to make you successful, it's lots of little things being done consistently.

Didn't win that contest this year? Apply again. Keep getting turned down from galleries? Ask them why, learn what you're doing wrong, and send out more proposals. Small steps will move you forward better than no steps, especially if you have limited time. Just stay consistent and persist.

Failure is not a stopping point, it's a place to pivot to the next thing.

<h1 style="text-align:center">24
Putting Your Health First</h1>

This chapter repeats a little with the chapter on priorities, but it's so important I wanted to give it a chapter all its own.

Put your health first.

I'm not talking about most of the time, I'm talking about all the time.

Your health is your foundation. If you're not as healthy as you can be, you won't be as productive or as able to function. Take it from someone who's spent well over 1/3rd of her life chronically ill. Your health is important.

Eat as well as you can muster, put in an effort to be active if you are able, and give yourself some mental health days.

This past fall, I had a ridiculous amount of stress. On top of my normal issues with my illnesses, which causes plenty of stress by itself, my fiancé was laid off from work. We had just moved, so we didn't have much money saved, and suddenly my artwork was the only thing bringing in an income.

Not to mention my father being sick in the hospital, my sister and her toddler fighting one cold or flu after another, my brother having job difficulties, and Daniel and I were feeling horribly sick, which turned out to be caused by mold in our new apartment and went on for months before we figured it out. I began having stomach issues, our new kitten had a limp, Daniel's car broke down, then his only computer he needed for training for an upcoming new job died, then my computer died, my phone was acting up, and it was just starting the beginning of the holiday busy season.

During this time, I had to make some difficult decisions when it came to my business and my own personal health.

I reached out to the media and was featured on my state's top news channel in their **Made In Vermont** series, which was great and helped bring in some bigger commissions and sales. The problem with commissions, though, like I said before, is that they're time and energy intensive for me to do. But with everything that was happening, they were still my best way to make the money I needed during that time. So I chose which ones I was going to do and worked on them one at a time.

Working on them one at a time meant that I could get one finished, have a happy customer, and get it off my back before moving on to the next. I was very clear with all of my clients that I could not work on a deadline and that it was a first come first serve system. Everyone understood and was fine with that, especially because I explained my health situation up front.

The thing about stress, for me anyway, is that you think you're handling it fine. You're working on stuff, you're being as productive as you can be given your situation, and things are progressing. But when you're stressing about things like financial stability and if you're going to be able to pay rent because of everything else that's happened, not to mention the amount I have to spend on medicine every month. That type of stress weighs on you even when you're not actively thinking about it.

Then you break.

It happens suddenly and it's a ferocious tide of emotion that spills over and destroys that nice firm "I'm just going to work my way through this" barrier you put up inside yourself until you're collapsed on the couch sobbing uncontrollably. What triggers it? Something little. You drop something, or cut yourself, or maybe it's a rejection letter. Something where normally you'd just sigh, clean it up and move on, but for some reason it is the last thing you can take going wrong and boom, you're a blubbering mess.

This happened to me. I was pushing too hard because stress was so high, and now I have the acid reflux (possibly an ulcer) and digestive problems to prove it.

Instead of trying to push through the rest of that day, though, even with one of my rare deadlines weighing on me, I went to bed and cried and then spent the afternoon reading a romance novel. When I woke up the next morning it was obvious to me that I still needed a mental health day, so instead of working I kept reading. I drank tea, I did some meditation, and I escaped into my book.

The second day I was able to do a little bit of work, but I kept it light, and then by the third day, I was back in business and being productive again.

If I'd tried to push through, I would have suffered for it (and consequently, so would my work). I've learned the hard way what my limitations are and how and when I need to listen to my body. When I first became sick and no one knew what was wrong with me, I tried to push through and keep going. I pushed and I pushed, determined to force myself to function like a normal healthy person, and it made me much worse. My body was under attack and I wouldn't give it time or energy to try and heal.

If you need to rest, REST. Your body is telling you that for a reason.

Even if there's a deadline hanging over you, if you need to rest, do it. No one knows your body like you, so if it's saying I seriously need a nap right now, or I need to go for a walk and get out of the studio, do it.

Take care of your body so that you can continue to be productive. This means physical health and mental health. Sometimes you just need a day off.

Artists tend to be especially guilty of wearing ourselves out. If you're a parent or you work another job, or you're chronically ill, then you are limited in the amount of time you have for your art career. Therefore, your weekends and evenings might be spent working diligently at your art and business instead of taking that time to relax and decompress.

That all makes sense and there's not always a lot we can do to change this, but don't let it ruin your health or your relationships with loved ones, or your life in general.

If you're taking all your extra time to do artwork, I'm assuming it's because you love it. No one would work a job and then come home and work on something else for that long if they didn't love it.

But if you're not careful, you may start to resent your art business.

This happens when it's taking up too much of your needed downtime. If you need 9 hours of sleep a night but you're only getting 6 because you're staying up late trying to work on an art-related project, then it's going to wear you down. Sleep comes first. Without sleep, nothing else functions correctly, so if you know you're someone who needs a certain amount of sleep, try to get that amount and then you'll be more productive while you're awake.

Put your health first and other things won't seem so bad.

For stress I highly recommend meditation. It doesn't matter how healthy or sick you are, anyone can meditate and it literally changes your brain chemistry for the better and makes you able to handle stress and overwhelm and everything else life throws you a little better. You can look up many types of meditation and guided meditation tapes, but if you just want to make it super simple, focus on your breath. Sit or lie down with your eyes closed and try to focus on nothing but your breathing. Breathe in, and breathe out.

Your mind may start to wander to everything else you have going on, or that movie you just saw, or what you want for dinner, which is fine. Once you realize your mind has wandered, bring it back to your breathing. It may start to wander again and again and you think you're just not very good at this whole meditation thing. That's normal! Just keep bringing it back to your breathing and you're fine.

25
Ways To Avoid Burning Out

Something you need to ask yourself is: Is this what you really want to do?

Is being an artist and making a living from your artwork your dream? Or is it something that sounds good and you kinda like the idea, but that isn't really for you?

I don't say this to discourage you, but some people are better off leaving their artwork as their hobby. I don't say that often because I want to see as many awesome, thriving artists as can be, but if you don't like the idea of selling your work or doing anything that we've discussed in this book, then maybe this isn't for you and having artwork as a hobby is enough.

If that's not you, however, and you feel that yearning and drive to succeed and spread your art out into the world and touch the lives of your customers and clients, you're doing the right thing by researching how to be successful.

The reason you need to ask yourself this question is because if this isn't right for you, the amount of effort that goes into starting a business like this will burn you out and give you a bad taste for creating in its wake.

No matter how good you are to yourself and how much you put your health first, there are going to be times when you are severely stressed because of this job. Don't let it get to you! Give yourself a break and know that this type of business ebbs and flows in all sorts of ways. There's an ebb and flow financially, with the amount of stress, with how many exhibits and publications you have, with how much correspondence is coming in, and even with how much creativity you're feeling. It's like riding 7 roller coasters at once and they're all changing and turning in different areas and at different times.

There's no question that some days are going to suck. Maybe even some weeks. That's the way it is with any job, no matter how much you love it. You're going to have negative commenters and annoying customers who don't listen to you or who question what you're doing. You're going to drop things, break stuff, and have something go wrong during an exhibit. Things will happen at the worst time, you'll get rejected, and for a period of time, it may feel like nothing is going right.

These are the times you need to sit down and remind yourself why you're doing this in the first place and that everything gets better. This is an ebb and you need to keep pushing through to get to the next flow. It's peaks and valleys, and the more you build your audience and perfect your craft, the higher those peaks will be.

Here's a few other ideas that might help you keep yourself from getting bogged down:

- **Listen to music.** Music can be extremely powerful. It can get us excited, and it can make us cry. When I was a runner I would have a playlist on my ipod specifically for running, with music that had a good tempo that matched my running pace. I was a runner because I forced myself to be, not because I overly enjoyed it, so music was how I helped inspire and motivate myself to keep going. The same works for creating. If you're feeling particularly blocked or depressed or professionally lethargic, maybe some upbeat music would help. Find a good Pandora station or your own music that will help lift your spirit and get you excited.

- **View Other Artwork.** Sometimes all it takes to be inspired is to go to a museum or to look up artwork online. Viewing artwork others have created, especially in whatever medium is your choice, can be incredibly inspiring and help you get past a block. Likewise, looking up other artists who have succeeded with their art business can be inspiring as well. Look up artist blogs and artwork and interviews that will help you boost your own creativity or give you that extra excitement to continue on with your work.

- **Switch Things Up.** I'm a wildlife artist, but sometimes I need to take a break from my detailed, time-consuming colored pencil work to do something else, like paint a landscape or draw a loose nude in charcoal with my fingers. It doesn't mean I don't love my colored pencil work, it just means sometimes I need a break. If you need a break from what you're doing, take it. Loosen up and experiment with something new. You don't necessarily have to have it for sale or in your portfolio, or maybe it will be and it's part of a different section of your website. You don't even have to finish it, it's just to get you loosened up and working on something different to get your artist groove back in gear.

- **Interact With Your Fans.** Nothing will rev up your creative gears like interacting with your fans. They adore you and they'll tell you all about every awesome thing you've done and what it means to them. When you're self-doubting mind gets out there and is told over and over again how amazing you are and how much people love your work, it's bound to do you some good. Go meet people in person or post your artwork in friendly social media groups specifically for artists and revel in the glory of having fans.

- **Hang Out With Other Local Artists.** Feel alone and isolated when you're working on your craft and business? Every artist feels that way. Meet up with other artists for some coffee and talk about your artwork and business and what you're each doing. You might get some great new ideas, some good opportunities, and you might give an idea to someone else.

- **Do Something Totally Unrelated To Your Business.** Sometimes you just need a break and to walk away for a while. Go for a walk, or spend a day with your family. Read a book. Go on a day trip. Exercise. Clean your house. Watch a movie. Whatever will help you decompress and allow you to come back to your work with fresh eyes.

Burning out is a potential problem for any job, but especially creatives.

For some reason, because being an artist requires creativity, the outside world thinks that it just comes to us. It's as if they think we have a never-ending stream of creativity and motivation that makes our job easy.

Our. Job. Is. Hard.

Some people will never understand how difficult it is to not only be consistently creative, but to physically create artwork and then switch gears and promote/market and build a business based on that artwork. There is nothing about this job that is easy. It's made even harder by people not understanding how much work we do. And that constant tap on your creative energy and needing to be every part of your business can wear you out.

Keep an eye out for signs of burning out and catch it before it gains momentum and creates a snowball effect.

If you feel that you're starting to get burnt out, stop and figure out what you can do to spice up your inspiration and motivation. It may take a few minutes of talking with other artists or looking at their work, or it may take a few days of vacation from your work where you get some distance.

26
Making Time For Your Art

This is a short chapter, but it's a necessary reminder: As an artist it may sound silly, but don't forget to make time for your artwork or craft.

With a limited amount of time or energy and all of this work you have to do to build your business, sometimes your artwork takes a back seat. You may not mean to, but you don't always have time for everything and you'll have to prioritize, which means sometimes marketing will outrank creating new work. That's fine. Sometimes that happens.

Just don't forget that your artwork is the basis of your business and your audience expects to see new work. You don't want to let them down. You also don't want to lose momentum with progression in your craft.

As an artist, you don't necessarily have to create artwork every day (although some of you may want to), but you should try to work on your artwork consistently. Don't go too long between stints of creating.

Creating not only feeds your soul, it also feeds your business and your audience's hunger for new work.

The only way you're going to grow as an artist is to keep creating. Make time for your art.

Creating may not always be THE priority of the day, but it's always A priority of your business.

After reading a book like this, it's easy to fall into the trap of focusing on your business and building your audience. That's not a bad priority, just don't let all of your time get sucked into the business side of things. Remember, approximately half your time should be spent on marketing and the business side, which means the other half should be set aside for creating.

Because your creative time is such a priority and you don't want it to be minimized, make sure you don't allow yourself to be interrupted. Turn off the notifications on your phone and devices, lock the door if you have to, and focus on your artwork. Feel free to listen to music or have chaos happening if that's your working style, or work in silence if that's your style, but don't let life and the business stuff pull your focus away.

You'll feel more productive if you can give 100% of your focus to your process as you're creating. You may also feel a deeper connection with your work, more satisfied as you create, a sense of meditation, and find it easier to find a good work flow.

Keep in mind that your business is built on your art, it's what started this whole process, so make sure it stays the foundation of your business.

27
Managing Your Fears

One of the biggest things that will hold you back in your business is fear. Fear of rejection, fear of humiliation, fear that you're not good enough, fear that no matter what you do you'll never succeed….

There's a lot in this business to be afraid of, but don't let your fears stop you from rising to your business potential.

Putting yourself and your work out there for the world to see can feel like exposing your carotid artery to someone with a knife. You feel vulnerable. You feel reluctant at times and anxious. What is the world going to think of this thing that you just poured your heart and soul into creating? What if they hate it?

Artists and writers and musicians are all exposing themselves when they let others view or listen to their work. No matter what type of art you make, it's a part of you. It took your creative energy to make it and no one but you could have made it quite like that. It shows your own style, your sense of composition and artistic technique, and if you've branded yourself well with your art style, people are going to recognize that it's yours immediately.

There's nothing wrong with feeling vulnerable and hesitant when it comes to putting either your artwork or yourself out there for the world to see. That's actually good, because it means you're aware of your audience and you're doing something meaningful. If it wasn't meaningful to you, you wouldn't care.

Fear is normal. It's expected. But that doesn't mean you have to let it stop you.

Think about this quote, one of my absolute favorites, from Georgia O'Keeffe:

"I've been absolutely terrified every moment of my life - and I've never let it keep me from doing a single thing I wanted to do." – Georgia O'Keeffe

You don't have to be ashamed or guilty for feeling fear, that's totally normal. Just try not to let it hold you back. If you're nervous about meeting with a gallery owner, that's okay! Learn some techniques to help calm yourself down and then go do it anyway.

Here's a few coping techniques I recommend:

- **Yoga/Meditation.** We've already talked about this one, but it's great so I don't feel bad about mentioning it twice. Yoga and meditation are fantastic ways for you to help yourself focus on the present and not worry as much about the future or the past. They help calm and center you. Learn a few good poses for yourself for when you're feeling particularly freaked out about something and see how much they can help you.
- **Power Poses.** We talked about this too. Take a couple minutes standing like you're superman and it will drop your cortisol levels and raise your testosterone, helping you calm down and be more confident. It's a win-win.
- **Write Things Down.** Have a whole number of things that are making you stressed or nervous? Write them down. Get them out of your system by writing down a whole list of everything you're freaking out about, and why it's making you so nervous. What's the worst that could happen?
- **Visualize Success.** Going for an interview? Visualize it going well in your head. Think about some of the questions they might ask and picture yourself sitting

there answering them in concise, articulate sentences. This has been shown to be hugely successful for helping people get over their fears. If you're going to be giving a speech, not only should you practice, you should visualize the whole scenario in your head. While you're driving to the grocery store or going for a walk, visualize the whole crowd in front of you and think about what you'd say, your body language, how the crowd might respond.

- **Visualize Failure.** It's the same as above, except instead of picturing yourself being articulate and great, you picture yourself fumbling your words and screwing up. This seems counterintuitive, but if you visualize yourself screwing up something like a speech, you'll be more prepared in case something does go wrong. If you fumble your words, stop, look at the crowd with a little grin (it's okay to make mistakes and laugh at yourself), and say "whoops, let's try that again," or something similar. If you mess up, the best way to gain back your confidence and that of your audience is to acknowledge your mistake, laugh about it, and move on. So picture that happening and you might be more prepared if it actually does, instead of fumbling for how to gloss over the mistake and pretend it didn't happen. The other benefit of visualizing the potential screw ups is that it allows you to picture what might happen if something goes wrong. Is it really that bad? If you say the wrong word, is it the end of the world? Or is it more minor than what your brain is making it out to be?
- **Sing.** This may sound silly, but studies have shown that singing boosts your endorphins and makes you happier, which in turn makes you more relaxed. So if you have to drive to your interview, sing on the way there. Loud and proud, and increase those endorphins.
- **Listen To Music.** Again, find music that pumps you

up! Or maybe some classical music to calm you down. Whatever works for you.

- **Go Outside.** Studies have also shown that being outdoors increases endorphins, boosts your immune system, helps you sleep better by adjusting your circadian rhythm, and more. So the thing you might need most is to go sit out on your deck for a while. Or if it's freezing out and that sounds like a terrible idea, get some music that consists of nature noises, as it has a similar effect.

- **Exercise.** Endorphins, circulation, overall health, etc. Exercise is good for you and will help with everything, if you have the energy for it. Go for a walk. Play a sport. Do yoga. Run. Hike. Play with your kids. Do yard work. Lift weights. Whatever is your preferred type of exercise, do it and try to do it regularly.

- **Do Your Research.** One way to be less fearful is if you have all the facts. If you're about to meet with a gallery owner, do your research and learn as much as you can about that gallery and that person. Not only will they be impressed with how much you know and it will make you look great, you'll be more confident going into it.

- **Retrain Your Brain.** We talked about this before too, but if you can try to retrain your brain to recognize fear as excitement, that can go a long way. Fear and excitement are very similar and in both cases your body is going into overdrive to help you function at optimum capacity. Embrace it.

Not only is there a fear of failure, where you think about all the things that could go wrong and what you're going to do if nothing goes right, there's also a fear of success.

This is especially common for those of us with limited time or energy, because if we start getting too successful and the business really takes off, will we have the time or energy needed to sustain it? What if you suddenly get so many commission requests that you can't do them and you're spending every waking hour drawing commissions and you're strung out? What if you have so many orders to fill that you're spending all your time packing and shipping and have no time for your actual business and artwork?

I'm limited because of my illness right now, so I can only grow my business in certain ways before it becomes overwhelming. I know that. Eventually, when my treatment has been going for longer and I'm feeling close to a normal amount of healthy, that may be different, but for right now I have to be very strategic in my growth. Passive income is the best way (for anyone) to grow and I have to limit the amount of projects that take a significant amount of my time and energy.

You need to decide what you want to do with your business, what you like doing most, and how you want to grow. If success scares you, it might be because right now you wouldn't have the time to do everything required to keep the business afloat. There are businesses all over that have failed because they grew too quickly and couldn't support a sudden burst in sales.

There's a few things you can do here.

For one, you can work on more things that will give you passive income, like digital products.

Secondly, you can work on promoting things that don't need YOU to do them. For example, if you sell reproductions and that's what starts taking off and you're spending all your time putting in those orders and packing and shipping prints, then that's silly. That's something you could delegate by hiring someone to do it for you. You could hire someone to do craft fairs for you, if that's making you a lot of money but you don't have the time. What you can't hire someone for is helping you with commissions or the actual drawing process. So if your commissions is what takes off, you can't hire anyone to help take over that part and lighten your load that way, but you could potentially hire someone to take over your marketing for you or other aspects of your business while you focus on the commissions, as long as they're bringing in enough money for you to be able to do that.

The more you grow, the more you can hire people to help you out in certain areas, and eventually you might have a whole team of assistants. Or you might have a business model you figured out where it can be easily run with just you, and that way you get all the profits.

Either way, success means changes are going to happen. Your already busy schedule is going to get jam-packed with everything you need to do and an overwhelming amount of correspondence and people asking you for favors and you needing to spend more time on shipping and meeting with clients and handling everything that's being thrown at you.

Don't freak out. Use the methods described above to help you calm down and then plan out how you're going to handle everything that's happening. Success is good! This is what you've been working toward, right? This is what you wanted! But you need to be prepared. Don't let your customers down by getting overwhelmed and not being able to meet their expectations.

Think of your business like a crustacean. Crustaceans, like crabs and lobsters, live in hard shells, but they're constantly growing. As time goes on, that shell is becoming tighter and tighter and pressure is building. When this happens, they're getting uncomfortable. There's too much in the shell and not enough room. Soon they're too big for their shell, so they have to shed that one and build a bigger one where they're more comfortable. But then they keep growing and eventually that shell will be too small for them too, and the process repeats itself.

This is exactly what your business is doing. You're in a certain sized shell right now, and it's comfortable. You have a routine and maybe you can do everything yourself without too much of a problem. But as your business grows, your shell is going to feel tighter. Suddenly you don't have as much time to do everything and you're getting panicked. You're rushing and overwhelmed. Something has to change and you have to adapt to the situation.

So you hire someone, or you tweak your business towards

more passive income, or you tweak the other parts of your life so that you have more time to spend on your art business, and that's your transition into a bigger shell where you feel more comfortable again.

No matter how well you plan, those transition stages are not necessarily going to be pleasant. The only reason a crustacean leaves its shell is because it can't live there anymore. It doesn't have a choice, it has to grow and make a new shell to survive.

This might happen with your business too. If you're doing everything right, then your business will grow and you'll have a period of time where you're uncomfortable. Then you have to analyze the situation and make a change.

Success can also bring on the fear that someday someone will look at you and realize you're a fraud.

As artists it seems to be par for the course that we feel like frauds. As success starts to happen and people are complimenting you and asking you to teach workshops and be interviewed, sometimes what runs through your head is, why are they asking *me?*

You're now an expert in your field, whether you feel that way or not, and people are going to want your opinion. They're going to want you to act like the professional you are even though sometimes you feel like you still don't have anything figured out. It's like turning into an adult all over again. You finally move out of your parent's house and into your own apartment, with a job, but you don't feel like you're really getting this 'adulting' thing down very well. Bills are nearly higher than your income, you try to eat healthy but fail half the time, your favorite thing is Netflix, and you're still not sure when you'll ever pay off those student loans. Technically you're an adult, but you feel like you're failing. People everywhere seem to have it together way more than you, and yet people are asking *you* for advice and treating you like a perfect adult. Is it in your head? No, it's just that no one told you the reality of being an adult. Sometimes it sucks. Bills are high and sometimes just getting by can mean you're a huge success. It may be harder than you thought, but you are succeeding at this adult thing, despite not feeling like it.

The same can be true of your business. You don't always feel like you're succeeding, and yet people are coming to you asking for advice and looking up to you and calling you inspirational. They don't have any idea you feel like you're lost or how frustrated you are at times, but that's okay. You really are growing in your success and you are inspirational, no matter how it may feel sometimes. You rock! You're taking a job that is twelve jobs rolled into one and you're actually making it work. And so far you haven't quit.

Just like I'd love to tell every young adult that adulting gets easier, I'd also love to tell you that feeling like a fraud goes away and that everything gets easier. Sometimes it does, and sometimes it doesn't. Those are the types of feelings that come and go. You'll feel like a rock star one day after nailing a press interview or a speech or finishing a great drawing, and the next week something will fall apart and you're wondering if it will ever get easy.

The answer is, probably not. Certain things will definitely get easier because you've had so much practice, but nothing worth doing will be easy. However, just because you don't always feel like you're an expert doesn't mean you aren't successful and have a wealth of knowledge you can share with other people who haven't quite gotten there yet.

Listen to me when I tell you that I have multiple chronic illnesses. I have an anxiety disorder and my adrenal glands push out way more cortisol than they're supposed to, making me feel that 'fight or flight' feeling all the time. I was pretty much locked in a dark room for 6.5 years in excruciating pain and have had to crawl my way back into society. I've had to crawl my way back to just being me.

And yet here you are reading my book.

My life hasn't been easy and by no means did I think I would end up giving advice for how to build your art business, but here I am. I've created my own art business and have become an entrepreneur despite my health issues, despite my nearly-crippling anxiety, and despite everything else that could have held me back.

If I can do this, so can you.

I'm not some sort of crazy genius and my artwork isn't any more spectacular than a lot of artists out there. There's nothing that makes me any more remarkable than the next person, except that I persisted, past my fears, keeping my limitations in mind, and strategized a way to be successful with my business.

- **Know your limitations and build your business foundation according to those limitations.**
- **Prioritize your time and energy on things that will move your business forward.**
- **Focus on passive income, and things you can delegate and eventually hire out.**
- **Be persistent in a smart way.**
- **Take chances and put yourself out there despite your fears.**
- **Recognize how far you've come.**
- **Plan things out (but allow that plan to change and grow as unexpected opportunities arise).**
- **Break down goals to make them less daunting and easier to achieve.**
- **Learn your working style so you can be as efficient as possible.**
- **Take breaks.**
- **And always put your health first.**

As an artist, there's a lot of different ways you can go with your business. I hope this book has helped give you some tips and techniques for being as efficient and productive as possible despite any time or energy limitations you may have, and has provided you with some good insight into what it takes to build your art business.

Good luck with everything and feel free to reach out to me! As always, I personally try to get back to everyone who contacts me through my website: **www.corrinathurston.com**.

Keep an eye out for my second book: **How To Communicate Effectively - For Artists & Creatives,** as well as upcoming books like: **How To Crush Self-Doubt and Gain Real**

Confidence, and **How To Think Like An Entrepreneur - For Artists & Creatives.**

You may also want to check out the Facebook groups: **Art Business Unlimited** and/or **ABLE – Art & Business with Limited Energy**. These are pages I created for people to come together and talk about their creative businesses, get advice, share opportunities or just vent about what it's like trying to run a business and stay creative despite adversities. Come join us!

Bonus Materials

28

12 Questions To Ask Before Creating A Partnership

As you read in this book, partnering with another person or organization in some way can be hugely beneficial to growing your audience. When you partner, you can tap into the audience of your partner and get your art or products or services in front of a whole new group of people. If you choose your partner wisely, not only will that audience likely have interest in what you have to offer, they'll be more likely to follow up or buy from you because you're being recommended by someone they already follow and trust. Therefore, your credibility is already established for them.

Partnerships can be great for your business, but you want to make sure you pick the appropriate partnership, so before you agree to partner with someone, ask these 12 questions:

1. **What Type Of Partnership Am I Looking For?** Do you want to be represented by a gallery? Have your work in a retail location? Be a guest blogger on a popular blog? Work with another artist on a collaborative project? Do a joint promotion via social media with another organization? Hold a demo at a local business? There's lots of different ways you can partner with other people and companies, so think carefully about which

ones you want to do and how they'll help your business.

2. **Is Their Audience Right For My Work/Product/ Service?** If you're a landscape artist, there's not much sense in partnering with an organization that only ever promotes sculpture. Instead, pick an organization where you know the audience is likely to like what you have to offer. For a landscape artists, maybe certain galleries and retailers, maybe working with a publication for landscape art, maybe cross promoting with a conservation organization, or perhaps offering to do commissions for a land trust company, etc.

3. **What's In It For My Business?** You don't want to spend the time and energy on a partnership if it's not going to benefit your business. Make a list of the ways in which this could help you. More followers on social media? More people added to your newsletter? More traffic to your website? More credibility by being associated with this other organization/gallery/person?

4. **What's In It For Them?** A partnership needs to benefit both parties, so make sure you have something to offer them as well. If they're bringing you a bigger audience, what are you giving them in return? Great content? Entertainment? Your own audience?

5. **What Are My Responsibilities In The Partnership?** You don't partner with someone and just expect things to happen. You'll need to do work. The amount of work varies depending on what type of partnership you're talking about, but for any partnership, you'll have responsibilities. For a gallery, do you need to provide new work every two months? Do you need to create promotional materials? Do you need to promote on your website and social media pages? Do you need to show up in person for events?

6. **What Are Their Responsibilities?** Just like you have responsibilities, your partner has responsibilities too.

Make sure they know what those responsibilities are and that they're going to do what you need them to do for the partnership to work.

7. **What Can I Do To Optimize The Partnership?** There's doing what is necessary and expected of you, and there's going above and beyond. As an entrepreneur, you want to always aim for being professional and going above and beyond what people expect. Can you create a great press kit to send to media about this new partnership? Can you utilize your other connections to spread the word even more? Can you create bookmarks or pamphlets to hand out to people who come to an event? The more you can do to impress your partner and their audience, the better the partnership will be.

8. **How Long Will This Partnership Last?** Is this a one-time cross promotion, or is it a lifelong arrangement? Will you have a contract for one year, or will you just check in now and again? Are you doing something that can be done annually, or just the one time? You need to figure out how long the partnership is going to last before you start.

9. **Do I Need A Contract?** Partnerships can be tricky. Maybe you trust your partner wholeheartedly, and maybe you don't know them well at all. Either way, a brief contract may be a good idea, especially if there's any sort of transaction involved. When I do a commission for someone, I always have them sign a contract BEFORE I begin.

10. **How Will I Measure The Success Of The Partnership?** Remember how a good goal will be measureable? Well, partnering is a goal and hopefully the goal for each partnership is known before you start. Want to gain a larger audience? Great, but how will you measure it? You can look at number of new subscribers, new social media fans, and new correspondence and

website traffic (and hopefully sales).

11. **Can This Lead To Other Partnerships?** One partnership is great, but you're going to want to continue to have more and more over your career to tap into all sorts of different audiences and build your email list of customers and clients. Is this a partnership that might help you get noticed by another company you're looking to partner with in the future?

12. **How Much Time And Energy Is This Partnership Going To Take?** If you're reading this book, you probably have limited time or energy. As great as a partnership may be, you don't want it to take over all of your time, so choose one that will benefit you the most while also giving you the time you need to work on the rest of your business.

29
Q & A With Author
Corrina Thurston

Q: What made you want to write this book?

A: The year before I had the idea to write this book, I went to an art business conference in Washington, DC put together by the **Arts Business Institute** and the **Best In American Made** show. There I met the head of the **Arts Business Institute**, Carolyn Edlund, and founder of the popular blog, **Artsy Shark**.

As an attendee of the conference, I had the option to schedule a 15-minute business consultation with Carolyn, so despite some nerves on my part, I jumped at the opportunity.

I was Carolyn's last consultation on the last day of the conference and we had a great discussion. I talked about how I am chronically ill and therefore don't have as much energy as a normal person, so my focus for building my business was going to be on passive income and things I could do at my own pace. She thought that was great.

On my way home after the conference I received an email from Carolyn. She was inspired by my story and loved the ways in which I was approaching my business to try and counteract my physical limitations. She then asked if she could interview me for her

Artsy Shark blog about that exact topic.

Of course! How could I say no? So we set up a time for her to call me the next week for the interview and she published it on her blog the week after that. (That article is called: *Creating An Art business With Limited Energy*, on the **Artsy Shark** blog.)

The response was great. Turns out it was in the top ten most popular articles on **Artsy Shark** for 2016! Artists from all over the world who read that article reached out to tell me how inspiring my story was and how they've been suffering from a chronic problem for a long time and artwork is the only thing they love doing and if I could do it, maybe they could too.

This response got me thinking and realizing there are a lot of artists out there who are either chronically ill in one way or another, or who have full-time jobs and kids and other life situations that don't give them a lot of time for their art business. This can lead to feeling overwhelmed and frustrated, as we all know.

So after doing some thinking and some research, I decided to write this book. I didn't know exactly what the response would be, I just felt the need to write it. I planned it out over a two-day period, chapter by chapter, and then I wrote the majority of the first draft in 5 days. 5 days! The words flew out of me until my hands were cramping on my keyboard. It's like this information had been bottled up inside me and I had finally opened the tap to release it all at once.

Q: What type of artwork do you do?

A: I'm a wildlife artist specializing in detailed, vibrant colored pencil drawings. My drawings are bright, detailed portraits of wildlife and domestic animals, which are a subject I'm passionate about, and I love to use my artwork to bring awareness to wildlife conservation efforts. I often donate some of my proceeds from a piece to conservation organizations. Feel free to check out my artwork on my website: www.corrinathurston.com

Q: What's your own art business like, day to day?

A: When you're chronically ill, there is no such thing as day to day. Each day is different and depends on how I'm feeling. Usually I'll get up and make my morning tea and read and respond to emails as I drink my tea. Then I'll have breakfast and move on to whatever project makes sense for me to work on that day, whether it's a drawing, marketing project, framing, going out and running errands, planning an event, writing, etc. It depends on what's the biggest priority at that time and what I'm physically and mentally capable of doing that day. Then I take a break and sometimes I'm down for the rest of the day. Sometimes, it's the opposite and I can go for a walk and then come back to the studio and work on another project and be extremely productive. Then there are days where I don't get far past my morning tea before I'm putting my computer away and going to lie back down.

Q: What's your number one business priority?

A: This changes month to month and year to year depending on what opportunities come up and how my business is progressing. At this very moment, launching this book is a priority. Last month, filling out the paperwork to apply for two grants was the biggest priority. The two months before Christmas it's usually commissions and making products to refill my inventory of jewelry, keychains, mousepads, greeting cards, etc. for holiday sales. This summer, if I get the grants I applied for, my priority will be working on the project I requested the grants for, plus a new series of drawings I plan to do that are bigger than I usually work, focused specifically on endangered species.

Q: What's your favorite thing about being an artist-entrepreneur?

A: Oh my, this is a tough one. Honestly, one of my favorite parts is when someone views my artwork for the first time and I tell them it's done in colored pencil and then they look at me like I'm crazy, then analyze the artwork as close as their faces can get to it, and then look at me again and go "No way! Are you sure?"

I always laugh. Yep, I'm pretty sure.

It's great to surprise people by using a medium in a way they've never seen, and seeing the shock on their faces.

One of my secondary enormous goals (second to my hope to bring awareness to wildlife conservation and endangered species) is for my artwork to help colored pencil become better recognized and respected as a fine art medium.

Q: Have you written other books that might be helpful?

A: Funny you should ask! I've written a second book called, **How To Communicate Effectively – For Artists & Creatives.**

This book will go into detail about how to talk and write about yourself as a creative, and your work. It'll take a look at things like artist statements, bios, blog posts, interviews, public speaking, and presenting. It'll help you craft an "elevator pitch" for when you meet someone and they ask you what you do or what type of work you create, and help you communicate about your art in ways that has people coming back for more.

The whole point of communication about your art is to get people asking questions and yearning for more, that way they'll return to you again and again. Check out my second book to learn more about the best and easiest ways to do just that. There's a sample chapter starting on the next page for a sneak preview!

I'm also in the process of writing two more books: **How To Crush Self-Doubt and Gain Real Confidence**, and **How To Think Like An Entrepreneur - For Artists & Creatives**

30
Sample Chapter:
How To Communicate Effectively
For Artists & Creatives

What Is Effective Communication?

Good, effective communication is essential for any business. If you don't effectively communicate what you're selling and how you're different or why people should buy from you, your audience won't understand what you're about and will pass you over.

People buy from those they know and trust. Effective communication, whether it be a video, a blog, a vision/mission statement on a website, a product description, an artist bio/statement, a speech, or anything else, is what you need to build credibility with your audience and gain that trust. The more someone feels like they know and trust you and your products or services, the more likely they are to buy from you.

Effective communication is what converts your readers and listeners into customers and clients.

No matter what type of communication we're talking about,

it's effective when it gets the point across quickly. Take this chapter as an example; I'm not using a lot of backstory or unnecessary words to get my point across. Instead, I'm explaining in a plain, casual tone what I mean when I say "effective communication."

Getting the point across quickly is good for you because you don't have to spend time on filler and fluff, instead you can be efficient and concise with your words. It's also great for your customer because people seem to have less and less time to read or watch or listen to anything and are being bombarded daily with emails, videos, podcasts, messages, and more. It's well known that the attention span of a typical person is shrinking and you only have a matter of seconds to catch their attention.

Get to the point quickly in order to prove what you're saying is worth reading or listening to, otherwise people will lose interest.

The other part of that equation is being articulate. This is more difficult but equally important. Not only do you want to get your point across quickly, you want to get it across well. You could explain something in a single sentence, but it wouldn't matter or be effective if you're not articulate and people don't understand what you're talking about.

Some tips for being articulate and efficient with your words:

Start from the beginning. A lot of people get so engrossed in their product or whatever they're explaining that they forget to start from the beginning! Your potential customer might not know as much about your product as you do, which means you need to give them a little bit of background info before you jump into selling it. Maybe you sell giclee prints of your artwork. That's great, I love my giclee prints. But when you say you're selling giclee prints and quickly start explaining to people your framing and how it's ready to hang, they might have a quizzical look on their faces because they might have no idea what giclee means or why it's worth the price.

Don't jump around, keep it linear. Explaining to someone how you became an artist? Start from the beginning and tell your story in a linear fashion. Don't say you went to grad school, but you've been drawing since you were 4, and you went to college for it, but you were a graphic designer for a while after grad school, etc. The more convoluted your story, the less it will engage your audience. People like stories with beginnings, middles, and ends. (More on this in an upcoming chapter specifically for artist bios.)

Try not to repeat yourself. A lot of people don't practice speaking to people or writing and they end up saying the same thing in multiple ways. Your customer is smart, they will understand what you're saying most of the time. You'll be much more efficient if you think about what you're going to say or write before you do it and streamline your words to be most effective. If you don't have much to say, it's fine to keep it short and sweet.

Keep it short. For example, when people ask me questions I keep my answers relatively brief. I often get asked how I became an artist and the story is more complicated then most artists. In order to read my audience, I'll tell them the very short version of my story, which for some people is enough because they were only a little curious. However, I tell it in a way that indicates there's more to the story, which triggers some people (most people) to ask questions in order to get more info and then I know they're interested in the longer story and I have their attention before I take the time and energy to tell the whole, unabridged story. But you need to read your audience and give them a way out if they're not really interested in hearing a longer explanation about something.

Avoid the Ums, Uhs, Likes, and Sos. We all have go-to filler words. For a while mine was "like." Then it was "so…" or "and, um…" We use these words and phrases to give ourselves just a little more time to think of the appropriate word or sentence, or because it's a nervous habit. This is a hard habit to break because you're so used to it, but those words disrupt your flow and make your message less clear.

No matter what you're communicating, you're telling a story.

Don't forget you're telling a story. Whether you're describing a product, giving a speech about art therapy, explaining your artist bio, or sending a proposal to a gallery, treat it like a story. Stories are infinitely more interesting, and therefore create more engagement with your audience, than just being told something.

Briefly describe how something came to fruition, how you came up with the idea for something, or how's it's transformed over the years to something even better than what the first one started out like. Be brief, but give your customers something to latch on to that they will think about every time they see that product, every time they need your service, every time they look at a set of watercolors, etc.

Stories are best when they connect with someone on an emotional level. The best way to draw your audience in is by tugging on their emotions.

I was just listening to a webinar the other day about writing and self-publishing books. I listen to webinars and podcasts a lot when I'm drawing, and this was no different, except that after just a few minutes I had stopped drawing and was staring at the screen. The speaker, Chandler Bolt, was explaining what made him change his life around and want to help people write their own books. That story was essentially watching his friend fall from the mast of a cruise ship and die right in front of him, causing him to wonder if it had been him who had died, would he have felt like his life had accomplished anything up to that point. It was a powerful story, and being a storyteller by nature and having told it many times, he tells it well.

Now he doesn't just use this story for promotional purposes, which is clear, it just happens to be what triggered his life change and it's the type of story that hits you in the gut. He shares the story because he knows it could help his audience connect with him and perhaps give them a taste of that same feeling he felt. It was a traumatizing moment, of course, so I'm sure it's not easy for him to talk about. But he does it in a way where you don't feel like he's disrespecting his friend by using his death as a sales pitch, instead you feel like he's opening up to you and letting you in to his life to see his personal motivations, and you instantly trust him more for it.

You may not have such a dramatic moment in your life, but you have plenty of things that connect you to the people around you and your potential customers. It also doesn't have to be sad. If you sell bright crazy paintings, play on your customers' wish to be happy and playful like a child again. Nostalgia is a huge motivator.

If you've ever noticed, the best stories, those page-turners you can't put down, all have one thing in common: they leave you hanging.

Always leave your audience wanting more.

The best books tend to end a chapter right as something exciting is about to happen, leaving you in an anticipatory state and making it hard to stop reading because you want to know what happens! This is the same with effective communication, especially for any kind of marketing.

If you write a newsletter that explains what's been going on in your studio for the last month and what's coming up soon, don't give away all the information. You want to entice people by giving them most of the information, but making them click to your website or blog if they want to know more.

Don't do this in an annoying way where you break off at an odd spot in your writing and make them click for more. Instead, give them the information they need and make it really easy to click to learn more *if* they're interested.

For example, if you have an opening reception for a solo exhibit coming up soon, give your newsletter audience the information they would need if they wanted to go to it (location, time, cost, etc.) and a short description of the event, but then let them know you have a blog post explaining your behind the scenes preparations for the exhibit and a time-lapse video of one of the main pieces on display available on your website for those who want to know more.

If you have a book you've written and you're giving a speech on the same topic as the book, choose a couple of your most potent chapters to talk about in the speech, but then let your audience know that there's a ton more information in the book if they want to learn more.

If you consistently give people great content and leave them wanting more, you'll grow an audience of people who are dedicated to you and eager to read or hear or watch what you have to say next.

But keep in mind there are a number of forms of communication, including those that have nothing to do with words. The next chapters explain all sorts of communication and how to engage your audience and keep them coming back for more. We'll talk about all forms of writing (blog, emails, product descriptions, artist bio/statements, social media posts, etc.), speaking (videos, in-person speeches, teaching workshops, interviews, etc.), nonverbal communication (eye contact, body language, visuals, etc.), and more!

So keep reading in order to discover lots of tips for using effective communication techniques that help convert your audience of readers and viewers into customers and clients, and how to best present yourself and your artwork to the world.

About Corrina Thurston

Corrina Thurston is a wildlife artist working out of Vermont, USA. She's a professional artist, entrepreneur, writer, speaker, business consultant, and animal lover.

Corrina began drawing in 2010, two years into a chronic and unknown (at the time) illness that left her nearly bedridden, with a 24/7 migraine, severe fatigue, insomnia, body pain, brain fog, anxiety, and much more. She began drawing from the confines of her bed as a therapeutic outlet during her limited "good" time.

Corrina found that colored pencil was the best medium for her. She was shocked at the amount of detail and richness of color that can be achieved with colored pencil. Because it is a dry, cleaner medium, it was perfect for using while sitting in bed without making a mess, and the pressure she had to exert helped lessen the shaking of her hands.

In 2014 Corrina was finally diagnosed with chronic Lyme disease, Bartonella, IBS, Endometriosis, two types of pneumonia, Hashimoto's Thyroiditis, and malfunctioning adrenal glands. She's now on long-term treatment and is seeing (slow) progress with her health.

Corrina is determined to have her artwork and her business accomplish these three things in particular:

1. Help other artists build their businesses, even if they have time or energy restraints.
2. Help colored pencil be better known as a fine art medium.
3. Help bring awareness to wildlife conservation efforts. She routinely donates some of the proceeds from her artwork to conservation organizations.

If you have any questions or comments for Corrina, feel free to contact her via her website: **www.corrinathurston.com**.